BEFORE ABRAHAM WAS

BEFORE ABRAHAM WAS

The Unity of Genesis 1–11

ISAAC M. KIKAWADA
and
ARTHUR QUINN

IGNATIUS PRESS   SAN FRANCISCO

Reprinted in 1989 Ignatius Press, San Francisco
All rights reserved to the authors.
ISBN 0-89870-239-9
Library of Congress catalogue number 88-83623
Printed in the United States of America

CONTENTS

•

To John S. and Katsuko Kikawada
and Barney Roddy Quinn

"Before Abraham was, I am."
JOHN 8:58

ABBREVIATIONS

AJSL   *American Journal of Semitic Languages and Literatures*
AOAT   *Alter Orient und Altes Testament*
BOr   *Bibliotecha Orientalis*
CBQ   *Catholic Biblical Quarterly*
HUCA   *Hebrew Union College Annual*
JANES   *Journal of Ancient Near Eastern Studies*
JAOS   *Journal of the American Oriental Society*
JBL   *Journal of Biblical Literature*
JCS   *Journal of Cuneiform Studies*
JQR   *Jewish Quarterly Review*
JTS   *Journal of Theological Studies*
OR   *Orientalia*
QJS   *Quarterly Journal of Speech*
TS   *Theological Studies*
VT   *Vetus Testamentum*
ZA   *Zeitschrift für Assyriologie*
ZAW   *Zeitschrift für die alttestamentliche Wissenschaft*

INTRODUCTION

•

No thesis has had a more liberating effect on biblical scholarship during the past hundred years than the documentary hypothesis of the Pentateuch. It has taught us to perceive the Pentateuch as a mixture of literary layers of varying antiquity. The greatest drama recorded in the Pentateuch becomes not the explicit history that is narrated, but the implicit history of the Pentateuch's own composition. The formation of the Pentateuch itself becomes for us the most important guide to the evolution of ancient Hebrew religious consciousness.

Not surprisingly, this approach to the Pentateuch first came to the fore in the late eighteenth and early nineteenth centuries. Within this intellectual milieu, the documentary hypothesis was not an isolated phenomenon. This was the great age for the discovery of time: process, history, change were found everywhere, even in rocks.[1] And if rocks could be made to yield the story of their formation, then the Torah, with some coaxing, should tell its story as well. The documentary hypothesis was, in short, a characteristic product of its time—but it has also turned out to be much more than that.

Since its original formulation the documentary hypothesis has had its own complex historical evolution. A recent survey of that evolution has distinguished no less than ten separate stages.[2] The traditional designation of four layers—J, E, P, D—has been subjected to many further refinements. Some scholars have thought they could distinguish a separate stratum L; others have argued for distinguishing between E^1, E^2, E^3, and so forth. Of course, these suggested refinements, at least some of them, are easily enough ridiculed for their excesses, but such ridicule does not touch the central core of the hypothesis. The simple fact is that by the 1880s, as a result of the work of Wellhausen, the documentary hypothesis was supported by a broad consensus of critical biblical scholars.[3] And by the midtwentieth century, thanks to the work of other great scholars like Gerhard von Rad and Martin Noth, that consensus had become so strong that it seems virtually unquestionable today. Von Rad in the last edition of his famous commentary on Genesis (published not long before his death in 1971) could write proudly, "How can we analyze such extremely complex materials [as Genesis]? There is now no fundamental dispute that it is to be assigned to the three documents J, E, and P, and there is even agreement over detail."[4] His claim was, if anything, understated.

Of course, there have always been those who have dissented from the consensus, more often on theological than on critical grounds. Compared with the calm understatement of a von Rad, these dissenters often express their views with a shrillness that makes them difficult to take seriously. Perhaps the most persuasive of these voices in the wilderness is Umberto Cassuto. He offers many plausible alternatives to documentary readings of individual passages. And yet, even he concludes his own discussion of the documentary hypothesis with the assertion, "This imposing and beautiful edifice has, in reality, nothing to support it and is founded on air."[5]

This is mere polemic. The documentary hypothesis is supported by more than a century of scholarship—and a remarkable body of scholarship it is. After reading even a fraction of it, someone who had not already prejudged the issue cannot help sympathizing with the exasperation expressed by Cassuto's contemporary, Gressmann: "Anyone who does not accept the division of the text according to the sources and results flowing therefrom, has to discharge the onus, if he wishes to be considered a collaborator in our scientific work, of proving that all research work done until now was futile."[6]

Gressmann and more recent proponents of the documentary hypothesis (a virtual Who's Who of Old Testament scholarship) obviously feel that a rejection of the documentary hypothesis entails a rejection of all the scholarly research done under its aegis, and therefore a rejection of the cumulative results of more than a century's work. A rejection of the documentary hypothesis becomes tantamount to a rejection of modern biblical scholarship, a *reductio ad absurdum* for any but the most reactionary of fundamentalists.

And yet does a rejection of the documentary hypothesis really entail this broader rejection? Certainly it does not if we take the physical sciences as an appropriate analogy. In the twentieth century many of the most cherished principles of Newtonian science have been unceremoniously overturned. Alfred North Whitehead could write, "I was taught science and mathematics by brilliant men and I did well in them; since the turn of the century I have lived to see every one of the basic assumptions of both set aside; not, indeed, discarded, but of use as qualifying clauses, instead of as major propositions; and all this is in one life-span—the most fundamental assumptions of supposedly exact sciences set aside."[7]

These changes, however, were regarded by no one as having rendered futile all the physics done since the scientific revolution of the seventeenth century. It was precisely the developments within Newtonian physics that required the revolutions of the twentieth century. If the new physics swept away Newtonian principles, this same physics did so in order to fulfill Newtonian inquiries and aspirations.

A closer historical analogy might be more helpful. The same discovery of time that led to the documentary interpretation of the Pentateuch also led to a revolution in Homeric interpretation.[8] *The Iliad*, no less than Genesis, was now considered by some scholars as a mixture of diverse sources. And much of Homeric scholarship of the nineteenth century, the best Homeric scholarship, attempted to retrieve these original sources from the received text by focusing on its apparent inconsistencies. In Homeric studies Wilamowitz occupied the same position as his friend Wellhausen did in Pentateuchal studies. (Wilamowitz himself dismissed the received text of *The Iliad* as a "wretched patchwork.")

Remarkable is the degree to which these two fields of scholarly inquiry parallel each other through the nineteenth and early

11

twentieth centuries. And this makes it even more intriguing that they should have so sharply diverged from each other in the midtwentieth century. At roughly the same time that Noth, von Rad, and their colleagues were hammering out the detailed consensus of which von Rad was so justly proud, someone of equivalent stature within German classical studies, Wolfgang Schadewaldt, was profoundly challenging the documentary approach to Homer.[9] To be sure, there had always been doubters. Goethe, after first hearing of the documentary hypothesis of Homer, wrote to Schiller, "When all is said and done, there is more subjectivity in this business than they think." Schadewaldt's work on *The Iliad*, however, was enough to drive many a documentary critic to despair. As one of them put it, Schadewaldt's *Iliasstudien* "brought crashing to the ground a century and a half of German scholarship."[10]

Actually Schadewaldt's work was so effective precisely because he did not bring the earlier work crashing to the ground. He did not want to render it futile. He did not want to because it had provided the true basis for his own work. He accepted the observations on which the earlier scholars had based their consensus. But he used their observations to challenge their inferences. He began his own unitary interpretation of *The Iliad* with the very books 8 and 11 that had always been the strongest part of the documentary case. He showed, however, that these books were parts of a greater whole; it was just that *The Iliad* had a far more complex unity than anyone had previously suspected. And we would never have appreciated the extraordinary complexity of this unity had it not been for the century and a half of work by gifted Homeric critics. His work was inconceivable without theirs, much as the twentieth-century revolution in physics was inconceivable without the two centuries of Newtonians who tried to finish his system.

Recent collections of Homeric criticism (at least those published outside of Germany) no longer seriously consider the documentary hypothesis of Homer at all. The editor of one explains:

As late as 1934, Gilbert Murray could discover no reputable scholar ready to defend the view that a single poet had written either or both the Iliad and the Odyssey. Today, the wheel has come full turn.

A post-Freudian age regards the act of literary composition as one of extreme complexity. Where the nineteenth century editor saw a lacuna or interpolation, we tend to see the indirections or special logic of the poetic imagination. Our entire image of the mind has altered. The higher critics, Wilamowitz or Wellhausen, were anatomists; to get at the heart of a thing they took it to pieces. We, like the men of the sixteenth century, incline to regard mental processes as organic and integral. A modern art historian has written of *la vie des formes*, the implication being that in the life of art, as in that of organic matter, there are complications of design and autonomous energies which cannot be dissected. Wherever possible, we prefer to leave a thing whole.[11]

Of course, the fact that classical studies has long since passed Wilamowitz by does not mean that the Old Testament scholars are backward because they still agree essentially with Wellhausen. Genesis does have the appearance of a loosely organized collection of traditional narratives, while *The Iliad* most emphatically gives the impression of being a single narrative. Perhaps Wellhausen, unlike Wilamowitz, had just found the appropriate material on which to use the method the two scholars shared.

Perhaps, but an alternative explanation does suggest itself. The unity of Genesis might be subtler, less direct than that of *The Iliad*, and hence more difficult for us to appreciate. If that is so, then we would expect the documentary hypothesis to be able to hold out longer here because the need to see beyond it was less obvious.

What we can conclude from the analogy with Homeric studies (and more emphatically from the analogy with Newtonian physics) is that the issue of unity is not closed for Pentateuchal studies, nor is it likely ever to be. However imposing the consensus, the documentary hypothesis remains an hypothesis. Its formulation may well have represented the dawn of a new day for biblical scholarship, but days have their dawns and their dusks.

In this book we propose a unitary reading of Genesis 1–11. And we do it in the spirit of inquiry, not of polemic. This section of Genesis has played the same role in the development of the

Pentateuchal documentary hypothesis as the analysis of books 8 and 11 have for the Homeric. The documentary analysis of this primeval history has been the foundation stone on which all the rest was built. It remains so today, as much as it was in the time of Wellhausen.

For instance, the best recent introduction to the documentary hypothesis has devoted almost a third of its length just to the analysis of this section.[12] Contrarily, the best recent defense of a unitary literary criticism of the Bible, when discussing this section of Genesis, speaks discreetly of its "composite artistry."[13] Quite simply, the analysis of Genesis 1–11 is the most impressive achievement of the documentary hypothesis in its long history. We are, therefore, going to attack the documentary hypothesis at its strongest point, the point at which it appears utterly unassailable to most scholars today.

"To attack the documentary hypothesis at its strongest point"—this statement makes it seem as if we perceived ourselves as being involved in a military operation, assaulting some citadel. Actually nothing could be farther from the case. We intend to ground our reading of Genesis 1–11 on the many astute observations of the older documentary approach. We do not intend to deny the apparent diversity; we just want to seek a subtler unity within that diversity.

The first step in this task will be to observe carefully the diversity itself. We need to review sympathetically what the grand old hypothesis of Pentateuchal criticism has to tell us about Genesis before Abraham was. Let us start with Genesis 1–5.

Notes / Introduction

1. One interesting introduction to the intellectual history of the period is entitled simply *The Discovery of Time* by Steven Toulmin and June Goodfield (New York: Harper & Row, 1965).

2. O. Eissfeld, *The Old Testament: An Introduction* (New York: Harper & Row, 1965), chap. 23.

3. Julius Wellhausen, *Prolegomena to the History of Ancient Israel* (New York: Meridian, 1957).

4. Gerhard von Rad, *Genesis* (Philadelphia: Westminster Press, 1972), p. 21. See also Martin Noth, *A History of Pentateuchal Traditions* (Englewood Cliffs, N.J.: Prentice Hall, 1972).

5. Umberto Cassuto, *The Documentary Hypothesis and the Composition of the Pentateuch: Eight Lectures* (Jerusalem: Magnes, 1961), p. 100.

6. H. Gressmann, "Die Aufgaben der alttestamentlichen Forschung," *ZAW* 42 (1924): 1-33.

7. For this quotation placed in its intellectual context, see Arthur Quinn, *The Confidence of British Philosophers* (Leyden: Brill, 1977), pt. 4. An important contribution to the philosophy of science attempting to take into account the revolutionary character of its recent history is Thomas Kuhn, *The Structure of Scientific Revolutions* (Chicago: University of Chicago Press, 1964).

8. A good recent history of Homeric criticism is Howard Clarke, *Homer's Readers* (Newark, Del.: University of Delaware Press, 1981).

9. W. Schadewaldt, *Iliasstudien* (Leipzig: Hirzel, 1938). A notable addition to such unitary interpretation is Cedric Whitman, *Homer and the Heroic Tradition* (Cambridge, Mass.: Harvard University Press, 1958).

10. Quotations cited in Clarke, *Homer's Readers*, pp. 164, 282.

11. George Steiner and Robert Fagles, eds., *Homer* (Englewood Cliffs, N.J.: Prentice Hall, 1962), pp. 2-3.

12. Norman Habel, *Literary Criticism of the Old Testament* (Philadelphia: Fortress Press, 1971), chap. 2.

13. Robert Alter, *The Art of Biblical Narrative* (New York: Basic Books, 1981), chap. 7.

CHAPTER I

•

Before the Patriarchs Were: Genesis 1-11 as a Paradigm of Biblical Diversity

1

The most important clue that a plurality of sources lies behind Genesis 1–5 is to be found in the changing name for God. From Genesis 1:1 to 2:4 God is called "Elohim." Then abruptly, for no apparent reason, a new name, "Yahweh," is introduced. This was the name of God that would eventually be revealed to Moses from the burning bush, but we also, somewhat inappropriately, find it here, long before that revelation, in the stories of Adam and Eve and Cain and Abel. Only at the beginning of Genesis 5, when the generations of Adam are recited, is the use of Yahweh discontinued and a strict use of Elohim returned.

So: "In the beginning Elohim created the heavens and the earth. . . . and the Spirit of Elohim was moving over the face of the waters. And Elohim said, 'Let there be light'; and there was light. And Elohim saw that the light was good; and Elohim separated the light from the darkness. Elohim called the light Day, and the darkness he called Night" (1:1-5).

But: "In the course of time Cain brought to Yahweh an offering of the fruit of the ground. . . . And Yahweh had regard for Abel and his offering. . . . Yahweh said to Cain, 'Why are you angry?' " (4:3-6).

Then again, only a chapter later: "When Elohim created man, he made him in the likeness of Elohim," and "Enoch walked with Elohim; and he was not, for Elohim took him" (5:1, 24).

These shifts suggest that Genesis 1–5 is a combination of two original sources: one that uses Elohim exclusively, the other that also uses Yahweh. These two sources have come to be called by biblical critics the Priestly and Yahwist sources respectively. But the shift in divine names is only a clue that such sources might exist. This shift cannot possibly establish anything by itself. The names have to be a clue to deeper differences between the sections, if they are to support a documentary interpretation. But before we seek these deeper differences let us first explore briefly the difference between these two names.

Elohim—traditionally translated "God"—is the more general of the two names. It can just as easily be applied to the putative gods of other peoples as to the God of the Hebrews. Thus in II Kings 1:3 an angel orders Elijah to ask, "Is it because there is no Elohim in Israel that you are going to inquire of Baalzebub, the Elohim of Ekron?" Of course, the Hebrews were supposed to realize that their Elohim was the only true Elohim and that they should not go whoring after others. But the term "Elohim" was a general one that polytheists, and even sarcastic prophets, could use as a plural.

Yahweh—traditionally translated as "Lord"—was quite a different kind of name. This name would not have been known had it not been revealed to the Hebrews by God himself. This was, therefore, not a term they would share with the Canaanites. It was a personal name, not one that would be used in the plural.

Perhaps an analogy might be helpful. Elohim and Yahweh seem to have been different for ancient Hebrews much as God and Trinity would have been for a medieval Christian. Aquinas could use pagan philosophy to prove, or try to prove, many things about God. The Trinity, in contrast, was something revealed only to Christians, and ultimately a mystery even to them. There is the God of the *Summa Contra Gentiles* and the Trinity of the *Summa Theologica*. This analogy works fairly well.

When we look at Hebrew excursions into wisdom literature—that ancient Near Eastern equivalent of natural theology—we find the name *Elohim* consistently used. When, in contrast, we look at the specifically Hebrew revelations of the prophets (and their unyielding opposition to religious cosmopolitanism), we find *Yahweh* predominating.

18

Once we are sensitive to the difference between the divine names, a possible documentary interpretation becomes obvious. In Genesis 1–5 we have an older tradition of Hebrew exclusivity framed by more recent and advanced Priestly accounts. Wellhausen notes this point in general terms: "What are generally cited as points of superiority in Genesis 1 over Genesis 2–5 are beyond doubt signs of progress in outward culture. . . . In its general views of God, nature, and man, Genesis 1 stands on a higher, certainly on a later, level."[1]

This is obviously a plausible explanation of the shifts, but not the only one consistent with the evidence, at least the evidence we have seen so far. After all, a single author, Thomas Aquinas, could use either God or Trinity depending on the context—and also could combine these two into God the Holy Trinity, much as *Elohim* and *Yahweh* are combined into the *Lord God* in some places in Genesis 2–4. In other words, Genesis 1–5 might just have an author with a strong sense of decorum about the use of divine names. When discussing aspects of primeval history appropriate to wisdom literature, he would use *Elohim;* when dealing with those aspects emphasizing specific revelations he would feel inclined to introduce *Yahweh*.

Divergent traditions or a decorous author—the divine names themselves do not permit us to decide between these two alternative accounts.[2] If this were all that could be adduced in favor of the documentary hypothesis, it would be only an interesting speculation. But this is just the beginning.

The change in divine names is paralleled by other changes in vocabulary. *Bārā'* ("created"), the distinctive verb of Genesis 1–2:4, is replaced in Genesis 2:5–4:26 by *yāsar* ("formed"), but then reappears in Genesis 5:1. In both Genesis 1 and 5 man is made in the "image and likeness" of God, whereas in between he is described only as a "living being"; "male and female" in the frame sections becomes "man and woman" in the middle. "Hā'ādām" in the creation account refers to humanity in general, whereas in the Eden story it becomes the personal name of the first man.

Vocabulary changes are themselves but local manifestations of broader stylistic contrasts. The Elohim sections are organized formulaically. Each of the six days of creation follows almost the same form. God says let there be, it was so; he sees that it is good, and gives it a name, and there was evening and morning of that day. And the genealogies of chapter 5 are, if anything, even more ritualized. In both sections the repetitions make the narratives seem dignified, if hardly exciting. And this is consistent with Elohim as he is revealed in Genesis 1–2:3, the transcendent lawgiver of the universe which he rules by his word.

The Yahwist section could scarcely read more differently. Here, rather than formulas, we have colorful human dramas, dramas in which Yahweh himself is a member of the cast. Yahweh walks in the garden in the cool of the day, holds conversations with his human creatures, even worries (for instance, that man "has become like one of us"). Actually, in these sections it is Yahweh who has become like one of *us*. In short, the contrasting styles of narrative seem to express contrasting conceptions of God. Apparently, the divergent traditions had incompatible theologies.

We might think it strange that an ancient editor would not have felt uneasy about these apparent inconsistencies. However, the implicit theological contradictions within Genesis 1–5 fade before explicit factual contradictions. For instance, both man and plants seem to have been created twice. Or, more precisely, man is first created, then formed—and the plants were first created three days before man's creation, and then once again shortly after his formation. An editor who would not worry about such simple problems within the narrative could scarcely be expected to worry about deeper conceptual issues.

So what we find in Genesis 1–5 are not only changes in vocabulary, narrative styles, and theologies, but also unnecessary, even contradictory repetitions—and all these obey the general sectioning of Genesis 1–5 suggested by the divine names. Of course, if we have predetermined to save the unity of Genesis 1–5 at all costs, we can explain each of these anomalies away. Perhaps only part of the plant kingdom was created on day three, and the rest the next week. Perhaps an ancient Near Eastern audience would not have felt a double-creation of man to be a contradiction. Perhaps we are dealing with an author so sophisticated that he would vary his complete narrative style (and theology?) from section to section. Perhaps, perhaps,

perhaps. But why bother with these interpretative gymnastics when the documentary hypothesis can account for all these anomalies with such ease, economy, and grace?

2

If Genesis 1–5 is the product of a single author, then that author is capable of two quite different narrative styles and has no compunction about using them to express two quite different conceptions of God. He would be a very sophisticated author, indeed. Presumably he would think that his two apparently divergent theologies were ultimately reconcilable. From his thesis and antithesis we would expect him to attempt a synthesis, a synthesis that would exhibit to an even greater degree his theological profundity and literary virtuosity. If we could find a story in which such a synthesis was achieved, then we would have the strongest possible argument in favor of a unitary reading and against the documentary hypothesis. And the closer this story was to Genesis 1–5, the better.

The story that at first seems to meet our requirements could not in fact be any closer to Genesis 1–5, for it is the story of Noah that occupies Genesis 6–10 and dominates the latter half of the primeval history.

The narrator of that story moves easily back and forth from Elohim to Yahweh, from an immanently anthropomorphic God to a supremely transcendent lawgiver, from formulaic expression to human drama. All the contrasts found earlier between separate sections are here together in a single story of considerable charm and power. The documentary hypothesis drowns in the flood—or so it seems.

Actually, the documentary hypothesis had its own Noah, and his name was Wellhausen. Perhaps Wellhausen's greatest achievement was to show how the Noah story could be transformed from a decisive defeat into a decisive triumph for the documentary hypothesis.[3] E. A. Speiser summarizes how this transformation was achieved in his own much praised 1964 commentary on Genesis: "The received biblical account of the Flood is beyond reasonable doubt a composite narrative. . . . Here the two strands have become intertwined, the end result being a skillful and intricate patchwork. Nevertheless—and this is indicative of the great reverence with which the components were handled—the underlying versions, though cut up and rearranged, were not altered in themselves."[4]

The last sentence of this quotation is the key to why the documentary argument at this point is not circular. The claim is that the *two* flood accounts, although patched together, have been each kept intact. Hence each account can be almost completely recovered from the received text, and each of these will have a greater unity and coherence than the story as a whole.[5] The claim is clear and germane—and the concrete textual argument in its favor is utterly stunning.

We must look at it in some detail. The Yahwist version is reproduced in the right column, and what has come to be called the Priestly version is on the left.[6]

6:9 These are the generations of Noah. Noah was a righteous man, blameless in his generation; Noah walked with God. [10]And Noah had three sons, Shem, Ham, and Japheth.
[11]Now the earth was corrupt in God's sight, and the earth was filled with violence. [12]And God saw the earth, and behold, it was corrupt; for all flesh had corrupted their way upon the earth. [13]And God said to Noah, "I have determined to make an end of all flesh; for the earth is filled with violence through them; behold, I will destroy them with the earth."

6:5 The Lord saw that the wickedness of man was great in the earth, and that every imagination of the thoughts of his heart was only evil continually. [6]And the Lord was sorry that he had made man on the earth, and it grieved him to his heart. [7]So the Lord said, "I will blot out man whom I have created from the face of the ground, man and beast and creeping things and birds of the air, for I am sorry that I have made them." [8]But Noah found favor in the eyes of the Lord.

The Priestly account begins in its usual formulaic way. Its perspective is cosmic: all the earth is corrupt except Noah, hence Noah and his line alone will be saved; Elohim's announcement is a judgment of pure justice.

The Yahwist account, in contrast, starts dramatically with what Yahweh sees. We too see. And we also experience not just the feelings of men but also the sorrow and grieving of Yahweh. Man, not the earth, is wicked—and so man, and as an afterthought the other creatures, will be blotted out. Yahweh, unlike Elohim, excepts Noah from the judgment; however, he does so out of mercy, much as he before had mercifully mitigated the sentences of Adam and Cain.

6:14 Make yourself an ark of gopher wood; make rooms in the ark, and cover it inside and out with pitch. ¹⁵This is how you are to make it: the length of the ark three hundred cubits, its breadth fifty cubits, and its height thirty cubits. ¹⁶Make a roof for the ark, and finish it to a cubit above; and set the door of the ark in its side; make it with lower, second, and third decks. ¹⁷For behold, I will bring a flood of waters upon the earth, to destroy all flesh in which is the breath of life from under heaven; everything that is on the earth shall die. ¹⁸But I will establish my covenant with you; and you shall come into the ark, you, your sons, your wife, and your sons' wives with you. ¹⁹And of every living thing of all flesh, you shall bring two of every sort into the ark, to keep them alive with you; they shall be male and female. ²⁰Of the birds according to their kinds, and of the animals according to their kinds, of every creeping thing of the ground according to its kind, two of every sort shall come in to you, to keep them alive. ²¹Also take with you every sort of food that is eaten, and store it up; and it shall serve as food for you and for them." ²²Noah did this; he did all that God commanded him.

7:1 Then the Lord said to Noah, "Go into the ark, you and all your household, for I have seen that you are righteous before me in this generation. ²Take with you seven pairs of all clean animals, the male and his mate; and a pair of the animals that are not clean, the male and his mate; ³and seven pairs of the birds of the air also, male and female, to keep their kind alive upon the face of all the earth. ⁴For in seven days I will send rain upon the earth forty days and forty nights; and every living thing that I have made I will blot out from the face of the ground." ⁵And Noah did all that the Lord had commanded him.

Twice Noah is given instructions as to what he is supposed to do. Elohim gives detailed instructions as to the dimensions of the ark and emphasizes the covenant that will be established. The animals, two of each sort, are to be brought on board, male and female, much as Elohim in Genesis 1 created man, male and female. Birds and creeping things are singled out for mention, as are provisions for food. Noah does as Elohim commands him.

Now Yahweh commands him similarly. This time no specifications for the ark, but different specifications for the animals. Noah needs seven pairs of each, so he has to round up another dozen. The pairs for Yahweh are the male and his mate, much as in the Garden of Eden Yahweh decided that Adam himself needed a helpmate. Yahweh does not specifically mention provisions, but he does predict the length of the flood, forty days. For a second time Noah does as he is commanded.

7:6 Noah was six hundred years old when the flood of waters came upon the earth. ⁹Two and two, male and female went into the ark with Noah, as God had commanded Noah. ¹¹In the six hundredth year of Noah's life, in the second month, on the seventeenth day of the month, on that day all the fountains of the great deep burst forth, and the windows of the heavens were opened. ¹³On the very same day Noah and his sons, Shem and Ham and Japheth, and Noah's wife and the three wives of his sons with them entered the ark, ¹⁴they and every beast according to its kind, and all the cattle according to their kinds, and every creeping thing that creeps on the earth according to its kind, every bird according to its kind,

7:7 And Noah and his sons and his wife and his sons' wives with him went into the ark, to escape the waters of the flood. ⁸Of clean animals, and of animals that are not clean, and of birds, and of everything that creeps on the ground. ¹⁰And after seven days the waters of the flood came upon the earth. ¹¹In the six hundredth year of Noah's life, in the second month, on that day all the fountains of the great deep burst forth, and the windows of the heavens were opened. ¹²And rain fell upon the earth forty days and forty nights. ¹⁶ᵇAnd the Lord shut him in.

24

every bird of every sort. [15]They
went into the ark with Noah,
two and two of all flesh in which
there was the breath of life.
[16a]And they that entered, male
and female of all flesh, went in
as God had commanded him.

This section is the most intricately woven of the whole
story—and hence there still remain some differences between
analysts on the attribution of individual verses. (We have
followed von Rad.) Nonetheless, more impressive than the
differences is the general agreement that has been reached even
for as difficult a passage as this. For our purposes the passage will
help us see the reasoning involved in attributing a specific verse
to one or the other tradition.

Elohim is used both in verse 9 and the first half of verse 16,
while *Yahweh* is used only in the second half of 16—hence these
are to be attributed to the Priestly and Yahwist traditions
respectively. We should not feel hesitant about breaking up what
appears as a single verse. Verse 16a has the characteristic Priestly
phrase "male and female," while 16b has the charming Yahwist
anthropomorphism of God acting as the ark's doorman. Mention
of Noah's six-hundred-year age is typical of the genealogical
concerns of the Priestly tradition (6 and 11), as is the mention of
the firmament (11), which was created in Genesis 1. The Priestly
writer will specifically name Noah's sons (13), while the Yahwist
is content with a general allusion to his family (7). While the
Priestly writer might in his pedantic way want to specify month
and day (11), the Yahwist will be satisfied with proverbial
measures, forty days (12) and seven days (10).

That leaves only verse 8 and verses 14-5 unattributed. These
we can assign by context. They must go to different traditions
because obviously the animals are not going to board the ark
twice. Obviously the animals of verse 8 should board with the
Yahwist Noah of verse 7, and the menagerie of verses 14-5 ought
to be nipping the heels of the Priestly Noah, Shem, Ham, and
Japheth.

If the documentary hypothesis required so intricate a
patchwork elsewhere in the Noah story, we might have cause to

complain. We might complain, but we would still have to explain unseemly repetitions, such as the animals entering the ark twice.

7:18 The waters prevailed and increased greatly upon the earth; and the ark floated on the face of the waters. [19]And the waters prevailed so mightily upon the earth that all the high mountains under the whole heaven were covered; [20]the waters prevailed above the mountains, covering them fifteen cubits deep. [21]And all flesh died that moved upon the earth, birds, cattle, beasts, all swarming creatures that swarm upon the earth, and every man. [24]And the waters prevailed upon the earth a hundred and fifty days.

[8:1]But God remembered Noah and all the beasts and all the cattle that were with him in the ark. And God made a wind blow over the earth, and the waters subsided; [2]the fountains of the deep and the windows of the heavens were closed. [3b]At the end of a hundred and fifty days the waters had abated; [4]and in the seventh month, on the seventeenth day of the month, the ark came to rest upon the mountains of Ararat. [5]And the waters continued to abate until the tenth month; in the tenth month, on the first day of the month, the tops of the mountains were seen.

[13a]In the six hundred and first year, in the first month, the first day of the month, the waters were dried from off the earth. [14]In the second month, on the twenty-seventh day of the

7:17 The flood continued forty days upon the earth; and the waters increased, and bore up the ark, and it rose high above the earth. [22]Everything on the dry land in whose nostrils was the breath of life died. [23]He blotted out every living thing that was upon the face of the ground, man and animals and creeping things and birds of the air; they were blotted out from the earth. Only Noah was left, and those that were with him in the ark.

[8:2b]The rain from the heavens was restrained, [3a]and the waters receded from the earth continually. [6]At the end of forty days Noah opened the window of the ark which he had made, [7]and sent forth a raven; and it went to and fro until the waters were dried up from the earth. [8]Then he sent forth a dove from him, to see if the waters had subsided from the face of the ground; [9]but the dove found no place to set her foot, and she returned to him to the ark, for the waters were still on the face of the whole earth. So he put forth his hand and took her and brought her into the ark with him. [10]He waited another seven days, and again he sent forth the dove out of the ark; [11]and the dove came back to him in the evening, and lo, in her mouth a freshly plucked olive leaf; so Noah knew that the waters had subsided from the earth. [12]Then he waited another seven days, and

month, the earth was dry. ¹⁵Then God said to Noah, ¹⁶"Go forth from the ark, you and your wife, and your sons and your sons' wives with you. ¹⁷Bring forth with you every living thing that is with you of all flesh—birds and animals and every creeping thing that creeps on the earth—that they may breed abundantly on the earth, and be fruitful and multiply upon the earth." ¹⁸So Noah went forth, and his sons and his wife and his sons' wives with him. ¹⁹And every beast, every creeping thing, and every bird, everything that moves upon the earth, went forth by families out of the ark.

sent forth the dove; and she did not return to him anymore.

¹³ᵇAnd Noah removed the covering of the ark, and looked, and behold the face of the ground was dry.

Here we seem to have an important discrepancy in chronology. Of course, our attention is first struck by the contrast between the drama of the dove in the Yahwist version and the pedantic calendar countdown of the Priestly—a countdown ended only by an order from Elohim. Nonetheless, the Priestly Noah seems to wait a full year (a Hebrew year) before leaving the ark, whereas the Yahwist Noah after the initial forty days of rain waits only another three weeks.

There is some fairly close weaving done here, including breaking apart three different verses. However, there is no serious disagreement among analysts over this, and von Rad would even break a fourth. He would break verse 6 into two parts, and place the phrase "and at the end of 40 days" in front of 2b so that this section of the Yahwist account would begin: "And then at the end of forty days the rain was restrained from heaven." This certainly seems to improve the Yahwist narrative, but many critics will refuse to follow von Rad on this. After all, if an editor could make such small changes as this for the sake of sense, why would he not undertake larger ones?

9:1 And God blessed Noah and his sons, and said to them, "Be fruitful and multiply, and fill the earth. [2]The fear of you and the dread of you shall be upon every beast of the earth, and upon every bird of the air, upon everything that creeps on the ground and all the fish of the sea; into your hand they are delivered. [3]Every moving thing that lives shall be food for you; and as I gave you the green plants, I give you everything. [4]Only you shall not eat flesh with its life, that is, its blood. [5]For your lifeblood I will surely require a reckoning; of every beast I will require it and of man; of every man's brother I will require the life of man. [6]Whoever sheds the blood of man, by man shall his blood be shed; for God made man in his own image. [7]And you, be fruitful and multiply, bring forth abundantly on the earth and multiply in it."

[8]Then God said to Noah and to his sons with him, [9]"Behold, I establish my covenant with you and your descendants after you, [10]and with every living creature that is with you, the birds, the cattle, and every beast of the earth with you, as many as came out of the ark. [11]I establish my covenant with you, that never again shall all flesh be cut off by the waters of a flood, and never again shall there be a flood to destroy the earth." [12]And God said, "This is the sign of the covenant which I make between me and you and every living creature that is with you,

8:20 Then Noah built an altar to the Lord, and took of every clean animal and of every clean bird, and offered burnt offerings on the altar. [21]And when the Lord smelled the pleasing odor, the Lord said in his heart, "I will never again curse the ground because of man, for the imagination of man's heart is evil from his youth; neither will I ever again destroy every living creature as I have done. [22]While the earth remains, seedtime and harvest, cold and heat, summer and winter, day and night, shall not cease."

9:18The sons of Noah who went forth from the ark were Shem, Ham, and Japheth. Ham was the father of Canaan. [19]These three were the sons of Noah; and from these the whole earth was peopled.

[20]Noah was the first tiller of the soil. He planted a vineyard; [21]and he drank of the wine, and became drunk, and lay uncovered in his tent. [22]And Ham, the father of Canaan, saw the nakedness of his father, and told his two brothers outside. [23]Then Shem and Japheth took a garment, laid it upon both their shoulders and walked backward and covered the nakedness of their father; their faces were turned away, and they did not see their father's nakedness. [24]When Noah awoke from his wine and knew what his youngest son had done to him, [25]he said,

"Cursed be Canaan;
    a slave of slaves shall he be to
        his brothers."

28

for all future generations: [13]I set my bow in the cloud, and it shall be a sign of the covenant between me and earth. [14]When I bring clouds over the earth and the bow is seen in the clouds, [15]I will remember my covenant which is between me and you and every living creature of all flesh; and the waters shall never again become a flood to destroy all flesh. [16]When the bow is in the clouds, I will look upon it and remember the everlasting covenant between God and every living creature of all flesh that is upon the earth." [17]God said to Noah, "This is the sign of the covenant which I have established between me and all flesh that is upon the earth."

[28]After the flood Noah lived three hundred and fifty years. [29]All the days of Noah were nine hundred and fifty years; and he died.

[26]He also said,
"Blessed by the Lord my God be Shem;
    and let Canaan be his slave.
[27]God enlarge Japheth,
    and let him dwell in the tents of Shem;
    and let Canaan be his slave."

After the flood the Priestly Elohim establishes a formal covenant with Noah and his sons. Before doing that, however, he repeats his command to be fruitful and multiply, a command that was prominent in the Priestly creation account. As God of the cosmos, Elohim gives a cosmic sign of his covenant, for the rainbow renews man's status as his image and likeness.

Yahweh, in contrast, continues his anthropomorphic ways. He smells Noah's offerings, speaks with his heart, and promises regular seasons. Compared with the full-dress treaty that concludes the Priestly flood, this has an almost offhand air.[7]

The attribution of Noah's vineyard episode (9:18-27) to the Yahwist might seem problematic on two grounds: first, it mentions Shem, Ham, and Japheth—names we earlier regarded as characteristic of the Priestly source; second, it uses *Elohim*. Neither of these objections long survives scrutiny, however.

In verse 18 the names of Noah's sons are introduced as if the reader still needed to be informed of them, something that would only be the case in the Yahwist version. The difference in divine names between the two traditions is not that the Yahwist exclusively uses *Yahweh* while the Priestly writer exclusively uses *Elohim;* the Priestly writer does use *Elohim* exclusively, but the Yahwist uses both names. (Both *Yahweh* and *Elohim,* for instance, appear in the Yahwist story of Adam and Eve.)

Once these objections are answered, then clearly the human drama of Noah's vineyard belongs in the Yahwist tradition. And 9:29, with its precise dating, is a typical example of Priestly punctiliousness.

So now we have reached the end of Genesis 9, and the documentary interpretation appears utterly secure. Nothing in the final two chapters of the Genesis primeval history seriously threatens that security.

10:1a These are the generations of the sons of Noah, Shem, Ham, and Japheth.

²The sons of Japheth: Gomer, Magog, Madai, Javan, Tubal, Meshech, and Tiras. ³The sons of Gomer: Ashkenaz, Riphath, and Togarmah. ⁴The sons of Javan: Elishah, Tarshish, Kittim, and Dodanim. ⁵From these the coastland peoples spread. These are the sons of Japheth in their lands, each with his own language, by their families, in their nations.

⁶The sons of Ham: Cush, Egypt, Put, and Canaan. ⁷The sons of Cush: Seba, Havilah, Sabtah, Raamah, and Sabteca. The sons of Raamah: Sheba and Dedan. ²⁰These are the sons of Ham, by their families, their languages, their lands, and their nations. ²²The sons of

10:1b Sons were born to them after the flood. ⁸Cush became the father of Nimrod; he was the first on earth to be a mighty man. ⁹He was a mighty hunter before the Lord; therefore it is said, "Like Nimrod a mighty hunter before the Lord." ¹⁰The beginning of his kingdom was Babel, Erech, and Accad, all of them in the land of Shinar. ¹¹From that land he went into Assyria, and built Nineveh, Rehoboth-Ir, Calah, and ¹²Resen between Nineveh and Calah; that is the great city. ¹³Egypt became the father of Ludim, Anamim, Lehabim, Naphtuhim, ¹⁴Pathrusim, Casluhim (whence came the Philistines), and Caphtorium.

¹⁵Canaan became the father of Sidon his first-born, and Heth, ¹⁶and the Jebusites, the Amorites, the Girgashites, ¹⁷the

Shem: Elam, Asshur, Arpach-shad, Lud, and Aram. ²³The sons of Aram: Uz, Hul, Gether, and Mash. ²⁴Arpachshad became the father of Shelah; and Shelah became the father of Eber. ³¹These are the sons of Shem, by their families, their languages, their lands, and their nations.

³²These are the families of the sons of Noah, according to their genealogies, in their nations; and from these the nations spread abroad on the earth after the flood.

Hivites, the Arkites, the Sinites, ¹⁸the Arvadites, the Zemarites, and the Hamathites. Afterward the families of the Canaanites spread abroad. ¹⁹And the territory of the Canaanites extended from Sidon, in the direction of Gerar, as far as Gaza, and in the direction of Sodom, Gomorrah, Admah, and Zeboiim, as far as Lasha.

²¹To Shem also, the father of all the children of Eber, the elder brother of Japheth, children were born. ²⁵To Eber were born two sons: the name of the one was Peleg, for in his days the earth was divided, and his brother's name was Joktan. ²⁶Joktan became the father of Almodad, Sheleph, Hazarmaveth, Jerah, ²⁷Hadoram, Uzal, Diklah, ²⁸Obal, Abimael, Sheba, ²⁹Ophir, Havilah, and Jobab; all these were the sons of Joktan. ³⁰The territory in which they lived extended from Mesha in the direction of Sephar to the hill country of the east.

11:10 These are the descendants of Shem. When Shem was a hundred years old, he became the father of Arpachshad two years after the flood; ¹¹and Shem lived after the birth of Arpachshad five hundred years, and had other sons and daughters.

¹²When Arpachshad had lived thirty-five years, he became the father of Shelah; ¹³and Arpachshad lived after the birth of Shelah four hundred and

11:1 Now the whole earth had one language and few words. ²And as men migrated from the east, they found a plain in the land of Shinar and settled there. ³And they said to one another, "Come, let us make bricks, and burn them thoroughly." And they had brick for stone, and bitumen for mortar. ⁴Then they said, "Come, let us build ourselves a city, and a tower with its top in the heavens, and let us make a name for

three years, and had other sons and daughters.

¹⁴When Shelah had lived thirty years, he became the father of Eber; ¹⁵and Shelah lived after the birth of Eber four hundred and three years, and had other sons and daughters.

¹⁶When Eber had lived thirty-four years, he became the father of Peleg; ¹⁷and Eber lived after the birth of Peleg four hundred and thirty years, and had other sons and daughters.

¹⁸When Peleg had lived thirty years, he became the father of Reu; ¹⁹and Peleg lived after the birth of Reu two hundred and nine years, and had other sons and daughters.

²⁰When Reu lived thirty-two years, he became the father of Serug; ²¹and Reu lived after the birth of Serug two hundred and seven years, and had other sons and daughters.

²²When Serug had lived thirty years, he became the father of Nahor; ²³and Serug lived after the birth of Nahor two hundred years, and had other sons and daughters.

²⁴When Nahor had lived twenty-nine years, he became the father of Terah; ²⁵and Nahor lived after the birth of Terah a hundred and nineteen years, and had other sons and daughters.

²⁶When Terah had lived seventy years, he became the father of Abram, Nahor, and Haran.

²⁷Now these are the descendants of Tereh. Tereh was the father of Abram, Nahor, and ourselves, lest we be scattered abroad upon the face of the whole earth." ⁵And the Lord came down to see the city and the tower, which the sons of men had built. ⁶And the Lord said, "Behold, they are one people, and they have all one language; and this is only the beginning of what they will do; and nothing that they propose to do will now be impossible for them. ⁷Come, let us go down, and there confuse their language, that they may not understand one another's speech." ⁸So the Lord scattered them abroad from there over the face of all the earth, and they left off building the city. ⁹Therefore its name was called Babel, because there the Lord confused the language of all the earth; and from there the Lord scattered them abroad over the face of all the earth. ²⁸Haran died before his father Terah in the land of his birth, in Ur of the Chaldeans. ²⁹And Abram and Nahor took wives; the name of Abram's wife was Sarai, and the name of Nahor's wife, Milcah, the daughter of Haran the father of Milcah and Iscah. ³⁰Now Sarai was barren; she had no child.

Haran; and Haran was the
father of Lot.

³¹Terah took Abram his son
and Lot the son of Haran, his
grandson, and Sarai his daughter-in-law, his son Abram's
wife, and they went forth together from Ur of the Chaldeans to go into the land of
Canaan; but when they came to
Haran, they settled there.
³²The days of Terah were two
hundred and five years; and
Terah died in Haran.

The analysis of this section does prove a little more
complicated than we might first have expected. The Tower of
Babel is obviously a tiny story of the Yahwist tradition. We might
have expected genealogies, however, to be more a Priestly
concern, but attribution is not quite so easy.

Von Rad can find a complete Priestly genealogy with all the
formal fastidity that we have come to expect. What is left over,
however, does not have the unity we have come to expect from
the Yahwist. Von Rad admits this; he simply calls these Yahwist
texts "fragments."[8]

Clearly 10:9 has to be attributed to the Yahwist, for only the
Yahwist would use *Yahweh*. And as we follow out the information
about Nimrod, we do get Babel mentioned, which is all to the
good. But, beyond that, the Yahwist text is essentially just what is
left over after we have removed the Priestly formulas.

We must at this point be frank. The results from the analysis of
Genesis 1–9 are too firm to be threatened by some local trouble
in a mere genealogy. The editor who had done such a fine job
with the two Noah traditions is caught napping here. We can take
some consolation from the fact that earlier in the primeval
history, in Genesis 4–5, the editor has included two mutually
incompatible genealogies. (The descent of the same persons are
traced first from Cain, then from Seth.) We can conclude from
this that the editor did have two quite different genealogical
traditions with which he was working. Why he should choose to
include the whole of the Yahwist genealogy in Genesis 5 but then

33

use only fragments in Genesis 10 is a matter about which we can only speculate.

Beyond this, we have to make a general point. Any hypothesis, even one as strongly supported as the documentary interpretation of the Pentateuch, will always have some phenomena that remain problematic. The decisive test for the documentary interpretation of Genesis 1–11 *was* the Noah story. Compared to that, the genealogies of Genesis 10–11 fade into inconsequence. After working through the whole documentary analysis of Genesis 1–11—including the genealogies—we can no longer wonder why this interpretation has gained such wide assent. The wonder is how a unitary reading of Genesis 1–11 could ever be defended again, especially since any such defense will have to counter the Wellhausen interpretation of the flood story. Eventually we will have to reexamine this interpretation. But for now let us just look comparatively at the primeval history of Genesis.

Notes / Chapter I

1. Julius Wellhausen, *Prolegomena to the History of Ancient Israel* (New York: Meridian, 1957).

2. The inadequacy of the divine names as anything more than a clue for the documentary hypothesis has been carefully shown by M. H. Segal, "El, Elohim and YHWH in the Bible," *JQR* 46 (1955/56):89-115. He examined the shifts in human names between, say, the personal name of a king and his title as king. He concluded (p. 115): "Just as those interchanges of human proper names and their respective appellative common nouns cannot by any stretch of the imagination be ascribed to a change of author or source or document, so also the corresponding interchanges of the divine names in the Pentateuch must not be attributed to such a literary cause."

3. Actually such an analysis of the Noah story had been attempted since the earliest days of the documentary interpretation. Despite Wellhausen's historical importance, all the elements of his interpretation can be found in Herman Hupfeld, *Die Quellen der Genesis* (Berlin: Wiegandt & Grieben, 1853).

4. E. A. Speiser, *Genesis* (New York: Doubleday, 1964), p. 54.

5. Wellhausen, unlike his modern followers, was not so sure; he thought that while the Priestly account was entire, the Yahwist version had been "mutilated." Wellhausen, *History of Ancient Israel*, p. 34.

6. A model exposition of the documentary interpretation of the Noah story is Habel, *Literary Criticism*, pp. 28-42.

7. David Petersen, in his "The Yahwist on the Flood," *VT* 26 (1976):438-46, is led by this anticlimax to make some ingenious suggestions, which in turn reveal some of the interpretive resources of the documentary hypothesis. He thinks the Yahwist flood story is ineffective, given the standards of his earlier stories. He

suggests that the flood story did not fit in well with the Yahwist's general theology, so he included it only halfheartedly. Petersen concludes: "Why did the Yahwist fail to do justice to the flood story?—because he thought it a divinely ineffective ploy. The flood had solved nothing; it neither blotted out humanity nor washed them of persistent evil" (p. 46). According to Petersen this "lifeless narrative" of the Yahwist was interwoven with the Priestly version in order to neutralize its challenge to that version.

8. Gerhard von Rad, *Genesis* (Philadelphia: Westminster Press, 1972), p. 145.

CHAPTER II

•

Many Noahs, Many Floods: Some Parallels in Ancient Primeval Histories

1

The primeval history of Genesis does not impress the modern reader as a unified literary work, even a reader who has never heard of the documentary hypothesis. It seems to be a number of loosely connected tales, with genealogies intruding here and there. We can find certain overlapping themes and styles. But the primeval history as a whole appears to be more a collection of narratives than a single narrative. This is, of course, only the impression made on a modern reader. Ancient Near Eastern readers or listeners might have responded quite differently. They might have seen a unity that eludes us; the primeval history of Genesis might presume a kind of sophistication no longer common.[1]

Hard as it is for us to keep in mind, Genesis is, from the standpoint of ancient Near Eastern civilization, a late work. Even if (for the sake of argument) we accepted the traditional designation of Moses as its source, half a millennium probably separates the Genesis flood story from the earliest Sumerian version we now possess. Genesis would be as temporally remote from its earliest surviving literary sources as a twentieth-century English author would be from Chaucer, or perhaps from Dante.

Even if we turn to the Indo-European tradition, Homer's *Iliad* is itself a rather late product. We are reminded of this by a surviving scholarly gloss on its beginning lines:

Sing, goddess, the anger of Peleus' son Achilleus and its devastation, which put pains thousandfold upon the Achaeans, hurled in their multitudes to the house of Hades strong souls of heroes, but gave their bodies to be the delicate feasting of dogs, of all birds, and the will of Zeus was accomplished since that time when first there stood in divisions of conflict Atreus' son the lord of men and brilliant Achilleus.[2]

An ancient commentator has placed *The Iliad* into a broader mythic context unfamiliar to most readers of Homer today.

Some say that Homer found it in a story, for they say that Earth was weighed down by an excess of men, there being no piety among men, and so she asked Zeus to lighten her burden. Zeus first sent the Theban War through which he destroyed very many people. Later, again, Zeus took counsel with Momos, which event Homer calls the Plan of Zeus. He was ready to destroy everyone with thunderbolts or flood, but Momos dissuaded him from this, and suggested to him marrying Thetis to a mortal [i.e., to be parents of Achilles], and the production of a beautiful daughter [i.e., Helen by Leda], from both of which acts a war sprang up between Greeks and Barbarians, from which time it came about that Earth was lightened of her burden since many were destroyed.[3]

It is strange to think of the Trojan War as a divine solution to the "modern" problem of overpopulation. And yet the commentator goes on to quote from a lost epic, *The Cypria* of Stasinos.

There was a time when the countless tribes of men, though wide-dispersed, oppressed the surface of the deep-bosomed earth, and Zeus saw and had pity and in his wise heart resolved to relieve the all-nurturing earth of men by causing the great struggle of the Ilian war, that the load of death might empty the world. And so the heroes were slain in Troy, and the plan of Zeus came to pass.[4]

Clearly this theme was a commonplace within Homer's own tradition.

Particularly intriguing is the statement within the comment on Homer that Zeus entertained the possibility of controlling human population with a great flood. Nagler observes that in *The Iliad* the flood image is fused with the war. He writes specifically concerning Achilles' fight against the river god Scamander, and

draws a parallel with the Akkadian myth of a great flood and of
Atrahasis, the Noah who survives it.

> The river fight is best appreciated not only as a combat myth, which
> it is, but also as a flood story of the exact type that Sumerian and
> Babylonian documents have made dramatically familiar to scholars
> of Near Eastern civilization over the last two decades or more. This
> theme, as many others, has been adumbrated metaphorically in
> Book 16 (384–393), where the headlong panic of the Trojan horses
> at the appearance of Patroclus in Achilles' armor is pregnantly
> compared to a storm and deluge sent by Zeus to "decrease"
> (μινφει) the "works of men" because of their violent exile of justice
> from the assembly. Just in this way did Enlil send a deluge against
> mankind because of their raucousness, destroying the larger part of
> humanity—to the consternation of the lesser gods who become
> involved in various ways—and failing to annihilate the race only
> through the intervention of Enki, the god of the deep, for his
> favorite, Atrahasis "the very wise." The general resemblance of this
> myth to the present struggle of Achilles against the flooding
> Scamander, and the associated theomachies, is made more cogent
> by some surprising similarities of detail: the Atrahasis deluge, at the
> peak of its destructive violence, "bellowed like a bull" and in its
> wake the mother goddess is stricken to see that her children "have
> filled the river like dragon flies"; even so Scamander spews the
> dead bodies of Achilles' victims onto the Trojan *Zweistromland*
> "bellowing like a bull" (μεμνκὼς ἠΰτε ταῦρος), the bodies that
> had filled his streams "like locusts fleeing before a conflagra-
> tion"—both images are thematically important in both traditions.[5]

The Greek mythic tradition shares with the Semitic a concern
about overpopulation. The Greeks (although they did have their
myth of Deucalion) might not think of floods as an important
means of controlling population, as would those peoples who had
built their civilization along the banks of rivers. Yet the
fundamental concern about population is shared.

When we turn to the Hebrews, we find population also
important—but in exactly the opposite sense. The Hebrew God,
far from punishing man for population growth, is rather ordering
him, "Be fruitful and multiply, and fill the earth." This
command, so long familiar to us, is in its cultural context utterly
startling, as unexpected as the monotheism. Frymer-Kensky
suggests that this command to fertility represents "an explicit
and probably conscious rejection of the idea that the cause of the

flood was overpopulation and that overpopulation is a serious problem."[6] A command, which now seems a commonplace to us, was argumentative, almost polemical, in its original context.

Moreover, if some features of Genesis now commonplace seem strange in their original context, the reverse might also be true. Perhaps some features of Genesis now strange to us (and hence taken as evidence for divergent traditions) will become commonplace when placed in their mythic context.

Take, for instance, the double-creation of man. We find man created in Genesis 1, and then formed again in Genesis 2; we naturally assume that two creation stories have been combined. And yet when we look at ancient Near Eastern stories of human creation, such a double-creation is not unusual. We find it in the Sumerian primeval history of Enki and Ninmah.[7] This history was written about 2000 B.C., perhaps at about the time Abram was ordered by God to leave Mesopotamia to become a nomad.

The story of Enki and Ninmah starts at the very beginning of time. Only the gods exist; they must do all the work to carry vats and dig canals, and they complain bitterly about it. Enki's mother, Nammu, comes to Enki disturbing his sleep and informing him of the gods' dissatisfaction. She suggests that Enki fashion "substitutes" to do the work for the gods. He agrees, and these human beings are patterned after the "form" of Enki himself (much as is man in Genesis 1). Then, a party is held and Enki is praised by the other gods.

The second stage of creation in Enki and Ninmah occurs when these two become drunk drinking beer at the party. Ninmah challenges Enki to a contest; she will make creatures, and he will decree their fates. Ninmah makes six creatures who are weak in some part of their bodies, especially the reproductive systems, and who might have difficulty surviving. Enki declares a fate for each one that counteracts the weakness and facilitates its survival. Enki then says he will create for Ninmah, and she must declare the fate for his new creatures. He creates a woman with a uterus and apparently he impregnates her himself. From this union Umul is born. He is described as weak in all parts of his body and totally unable to care for himself. Ninmah is puzzled what to do with the creature. She says to Enki, "The man you have fashioned is neither alive nor dead, he cannot carry anything" (line 101). There are many indications that this creature Ninmah does not recognize is a newborn baby. As Kilmer points out, "The description is exactly that of a newborn; its eyes do not function properly, it cannot control its bowels, it cannot sit, chew food, etc."[8]

In the story of Enki and Ninmah, the creation of mankind to do the work of the gods is first described in general terms, and then recounted more specifically with an emphasis on the human capacity for reproduction. We seem to have in the second, more specific version, the ancient Near Eastern equivalent of the Original Sin; it was not the original human sin, but rather the original divine mistake. We know from reading comparable myths that the gods should not have enabled mankind to reproduce on its own, for humans will overuse this capacity and thereby become a burden on the earth and a nuisance to the gods. Some of the gods will begin to feel like the sorcerer's apprentice, and bad times—including a great flood—are probably in store for man.

If we juxtapose this story with Genesis, the Hebrew author seems to have put new wine in old bottles. Much as we have in Genesis apparent residues of the old polytheism ("Let us make man in our image"), so we also have residues of the old mythic structure. The Hebrew author would naturally suppress the detail that explains the need for a double-creation, for he is far from identifying the original sin/mistake with reproduction. But other indications of the older myth might still peek through, as when Eve says "I have gotten a man with the help of the Lord."[9]

Let us assume that the author (or authors) of Genesis 1–11 presumed that its audience would be familiar with the primeval history as it was usually told in the ancient Near East. This is not a very daring assumption, for the land of the Hebrews was often both politically and culturally dependent upon the great civilizations occupying the Tigris and Euphrates river systems. Not a very daring assumption but potentially a very illuminating one. If we could reconstruct the convention for primeval history as it developed in the ancient Near East, we might just be able to recover an important part of the rhetorical context in which Genesis 1–11 was composed. Then we might just be in a position to determine to what extent the apparent diversity of Genesis

1–11 is in the text and to what extent it only seems to be there because we have applied inappropriate standards of judgment.

But to build such a high tower—as any Babylonian architect could tell us—we need a much broader empirical base. We must start by examining the oldest Near Eastern primeval history that survives in relatively complete form. This would be the Akkadian version of the Atrahasis epic (to which Nagler refers) recorded in cuneiform by a junior scribe named Ku-Aya in the seventeenth century B.C. (approximately the time that the Hebrew patriarch Joseph is traditionally said to have lived).[10]

2

When the gods like men
Bore the work and suffered the toil—
The toil of the gods was great,
The work was heavy, the distress was much—
The great Anunnaki, The Seven
Made the Igigi bear the burden (1:1-6).

This epic begins by describing the prehistoric and mythological time when the gods had to suffer the toil of daily work. The laboring class gods, the Igigi, overburdened by forced labor in sustaining the managerial class of gods, rebel against these elite gods, the Anunnaki.

For forty years
The work they suffered night and day.
They [were complaining], backbiting,
Grumbling in the excavation:
"Let us confront our . . . the chamberlain,
That he may relieve us of our heavy work (1:37-42).

In response to this rebellion, the chief god Enlil and his assembly of gods ask the mother goddess, who is appropriately called Mami, to create man to relieve the working gods of their hard labor.

They summoned and asked the goddess,
The midwife of the gods, wise Mami,
"You are the mother-womb, creatress of mankind,

41

Create Lullû that he may bear the yoke,
Let him bear the yoke, the task of Enlil,
Let man carry the toil of the gods" (1:192-7).

She does this with the help of a magician god, Enki, who will
prove to be a great benefactor of mankind.

Mami opened her mouth
And addressed the great gods,
"You commanded me a task, I have completed it. . . .
I have removed your heavy work,
I have imposed your toil on man.
You raised a noise for mankind,
I have loosed the yoke, I have established freedom" (1:235-43).

Then follows on a very broken tablet a second, more specific
creation of human pairs to work and reproduce a more specific
creation account similar to that we have already seen in Enki and
Ninmah.

The newly created beings are so fertile that they fill the earth
and make too much noise for Enlil.[11] He tries to quiet the earth
with a plague.

Twelve hundred years [had not yet passed]
[When the land extended] and the people multiplied

The [land] was bellowing [like a bull],
The god got disturbed with [their uproar].

[Enlil heard] their noise
[And addressed] the great gods,

"The noise of mankind [has become too intense for me],
[With their uproar] I am deprived of sleep. . . .
Let there be plague" (1:352-60).

When the noise returns, he tries a famine caused by drought.

Twelve hundred years had not yet passed
When the land extended and the peoples multiplied.

The land was bellowing like a bull
The god got disturbed with their uproar.

Enlil heard their noise
And addressed the great gods,

42

"The noise of mankind has become too intense for me,
With their uproar I am deprived of sleep.

Cut off supplies for the peoples,
Let there be a scarcity of plant-life to satisfy their hunger.

Adad should withhold his rain,
And below, the flood should not come up from the abyss.

Let the wind blow and parch the ground,
Let the clouds thicken but not release a downpour,

Let the fields diminish their yields,
Let Nisaba stop up her breast.

There must be no rejoicing among them . . .
must be suppressed" (2[1]:1-21).

When the famine seems to be insufficient, he intensifies it.

The womb of earth did not bear,
Vegetation did not sprout . . .

People were not seen . . .

The black fields became white,
The broad plain was choked with salt.

For one year they ate couch-grass;
For the second year they suffered the itch.

The third year came
Their features [became strange] with hunger.

[Their faces] were encrusted, like malt,
[And they were living] on the verge of death.

[Their] faces appeared green,
They walked hunched [in the street].

Their broad shoulders [became narrow],
Their long legs [became short] (2[4]:4-18).

When even this fails, the persistent Enlil and his assembly try
to get Enki to exterminate mankind with a flood. He refuses.

Enki opened his mouth
And addressed the gods [his brothers],

"Why will you bind me with an oath . . . ?
Am I to lay my hands on my own peoples?

43

The flood that you are commanding [me],
Who is it? I [do not know].

Am I to give birth to [a flood]?
That is the task of [Enlil] (2[7]:40-47).

The gods go ahead with their plan anyway.

The gods commanded total destruction,
Enlil did an evil deed on the peoples ([8]:34-5).

But this fails as well because Enki gives shrewd advice to his
favorite man, Atrahasis. [12]

Atrahasis opened his mouth
And addressed his lord,

"Teach me the meaning [of the dream] . . .
that I may seek its outcome."

[Enki] opened his mouth
And addressed his slave,
"You say, 'What am I to seek?'
Observe the one task that I will address to you:

Wall, listen to me!
Reed wall, observe all my words!

Destroy your house, build a boat,
Spurn property and save life.

The boat which you build
be equal . . .   [2 lines missing.]

Roof it over like the Apsu.

So that the sun shall not see inside it
Let it be roofed over above and below.

The tackle should be very strong,
Let the pitch be tough, and so give [the boat] strength.

I will rain down upon you here
An abundance of birds, a profusion of fishes."

Of the coming Flood of seven days he spoke to him (3[1]:11-36).

When the gods realize that they have failed to exterminate
mankind once again, Enki admits he is responsible.

[The warrior Enlil] saw the vessel,
And was filled with anger at the Igigi,

"All we great Anunnaki
Decided together on an oath.

Where did life escape?
How did man survive in the destruction?"

Anu opened his mouth
And addressed the warrior Enlil,

"Who but Enki could do this? . . .
I did not reveal the command."

[Enki] opened his mouth
[And addressed] the great gods,

"I did it [indeed] in front of you!
[I am responsible] for saving life (3[6]:5–19).

In the fragments that remain of the epic, a resolution of some
sort is reached.

Enlil opened his mouth and
He said to Enki the prince,

[Come], summon Nintu, the birth-goddess
[You] and she, confer in the assembly."

[Enki] opened his mouth
And [addressed] Nintu, the birth-goddess,
"[You], birth-goddess, creatress of destinies . . .
for the peoples . . .
let there be.

In addition let there be a third category among the peoples
[Let there be] among the peoples women who bear and women
    who do not bear.

Let there be among the peoples the *Pāšittu*-demon
To snatch the baby from the lap of her who bore it.

Establish *Ugbabtu*-women, *Entu*-women, and *Igiṣītu*-women,
And let them be taboo and so stop childbirth (3[6]:41–3[7]:11).

So the Atrahasis epic ends. On the surface this epic seems to
have only occasional and inconsequential parallels with Genesis
1–11, but we must not judge the matter prematurely.

Scholars are in basic agreement about the structure of Atrahasis and its general intent. Jørgen Laessøe first suggested that the Atrahasis epic should be considered as the "Babylonian History of Mankind." He summarizes the major events of the epic in this way:

> The several Akkadian versions of the Atrahasis Epic present a history of mankind: from man's creation by the Mother Goddess, through his tribulations due to the anger of the hostile god, culminating in the deluge, from which man escaped only with Enki's aid, and thus secured a continued existence for himself owing to the survival of Atrahasis.[13]

This basic outline of the epic was confirmed by Lambert and Millard in their critical edition of Atrahasis.[14] They augment Laessøe's observations by recognizing three stages of increasing intensity in man's tribulations, culminating in the great flood. The tribulations are followed by a conclusion, which describes the post-flood compromise between Enlil and Enki. The components of the epic are designated as follows:

A. Creation	I. 1–351
B. First Threat	I. 352–415
C. Second Threat	II. i 1–II v.21
D. Final Threat	II. v. 22–III vi. 4
E. Resolution	III. vi.5–viii. 18

In addition to their five-point outline of this epic, Lambert and Millard also observe that the second threat to mankind is composed of two parts.[15] Thus component C is a double story. The population increases and Enlil tries to reduce it with a drought. But when the drought lessens, the population again begins to increase, causing Enlil to intensify the drought. This second part is not preceded by the usual refrain,

Twelve hundred years had not yet passed,
When the land extended and the peoples multiplied
(cf. I 352f., II. i. 1f.)

indicating that these two parts constitute only one unit and that the second part is dependent upon the first.

The resolution of the Atrahasis epic, component E, may well begin with another increase of the human population. In this component, however, the increase leads not to another disastrous death threat but rather to a compromise between Enlil and Enki. Atrahasis becomes in the last episode, as Kilmer points out, a plea for the practical solution to the population problem in ancient urban Mesopotamia.[16] Even though the text is not wholly preserved, we can discern at least three phenomena understood as maintaining population control, and the fragments strongly suggest that there were more:

1. Natural barrenness in, "Let there be among peoples, women who do not bear" (III. vii. 2).
2. A high infant mortality rate in, "Let there be among the peoples the Pāšittu-demon to snatch the baby from the lap of her who bore it" (III. vii. 3f.).
3. Establishment of artificial barrenness by cult practices of at least three types of priestesses or nuns, namely the *ugbabtu, entu,* and *igiṣītu* (III. vii. 6f.).

The sequence of events in Atrahasis is: creation; three accounts of a rapid increase in population countered by a threat of extinction never fully realized; and finally, resolution of the problem of overpopulation by birth control.[17]

When we place a plot outline of Atrahasis side-by-side with the sequence of stories in Genesis 1–11, we find some striking parallels.

ATRAHASIS	GENESIS
A. Creation (I. 1–351) Summary of work of gods Creation of man	A. Creation (1:1–2:3) Summary of work of God Creation of man
B. First Threat (I. 352–415) Man's numerical increase Plague, Enki's help	B. First Threat (2:4–3:24) Genealogy of heaven and earth, Adam and Eve
C. Second Threat (II. i. 1–11 v. 21) Man's numerical increase	C. Second Threat (4:1–4:26) Cain and Abel

47

1. Drought, numerical increase
2. Intensified drought, Enki's help

D. Final Threat (II. v. 22–III vi. 4)
   Numerical increase
   Atrahasis' Flood,
   Salvation in boat

E. Resolution (III.vi.5–viii.18)
   Numerical increase
   Compromise between Enlil and Enki, "Birth Control"

1. Cain and Abel, genealogy
2. Lamech's taunt (in genealogy)

D. Final Threat (5:1–9:29)
   Genealogy
   Noah's Flood,
   Salvation in ark

E. Resolution (10:1–11:32)
   Genealogy
   Tower of Babel and Dispersion Genealogy, Abram leaves Ur[18]

Remarkably, we can also find a similar structure in the primeval history of which the Trojan War was a part:

Problem = Overpopulation, wickedness, earth burdened.
First Threat = Zeus sends Theban War—many destroyed.
Second Threat = Zeus' plan to destroy all by thunderbolts or flood. Momos dissuades Zeus from this plan.
Third Threat = Momos suggests that Thetis marry a mortal to create Achilles and that Zeus father Helen of Troy.
This results in a war between Greeks and Barbarians.
Resolution = Many destroyed; earth lightened of her burden.

Note that in all three of these primeval histories there is a doubling in the second threat: drought and intensified drought in Atrahasis; in Genesis, Cain's murder and Lamech's taunt; thunderbolts *or* flood in the Greek.

Can we find other ancient primeval histories that also use this structure? The oldest Sumerian history, although it contains a flood story, is of little help because it comes to us on a single, broken tablet without any duplicate to help fill in gaps.[19] There are many specific suggestive parallels: creation of humans, multiplication of animals (though not of humans), institution of cities, a devastating flood foretold, one family saved by means of a boat, and a new era begun in which man's continued existence is assured. So we can say that the Sumerian author of this history

48

could begin with a creation and end with the optimistic aftermath of a flood, but we get no direct confirmation of a strict five-part sequence. Then again, we cannot say much about the structure of this primeval history as a whole, for less than a quarter of it survives.[20]

The Zoroastrian tale of Yima and the vessel of salvation is more helpful. It follows the five-part structure and yet adapts it to its own purposes. The tale of Yima is found in the second book Vidēvdāt, more popularly known as the Vendidad, which constitutes a part of the late Zoroastrian corpus of literature called Avesta.[21] In this tale, Yima is depicted as the first human being to whom the god Ahura Mazda reveals his religion. As is typical of Avestan literature, the whole tale is told by Ahura Mazda to Zoroaster. In response to the latter's question, "To whom did you reveal the religion of Ahura and Zoroaster?" Ahura Mazda answers, "To good Yima!"

At the outset Ahura Mazda tells Yima to become the guardian and cultivator of the religion, but Yima refuses on the grounds that he has never been instructed to be such a person. As a result, Ahura Mazda instead assigns Yima to be king, to make the world prosper and increase. To facilitate this undertaking, Yima is given two instruments, a golden goad and a gold-inlaid whip. Indeed he was successful at his task, as we read in the text:

Then passed 300 years of Yima's kingship.
Then for him the earth became full
Of small and large cattle and men
And dogs and birds
And the red burning fire.
The small and large cattle and men
Did not find enough room.

Yima, by using the golden goad and the gold-inlaid whip, makes the earth goddess Armaiti expand herself in order to accommodate the increase. The earth expands by one-third of her original size.

Then another period of three hundred years passes, and the earth again becomes too small for all creatures; so earth is expanded again by one-third. In this fashion, after a period of nine hundred years, the earth becomes twice her original size, while the small and large cattle and men and dogs and birds and the red burning fire become ever more prosperous and numerous.

At this point in the story the creator Ahura Mazda invokes an assembly of important gods. Subsequently, Ahura Mazda warns Yima that a dreadful and deadly winter will come with an extraordinary snowfall and that Yima should make a *vara* or enclosure, in the form of a three-storied cube having a door and a window. Yima is instructed also to bring into the *vara* the seeds of the best small and large cattle and men and dogs and birds and the red burning fire. Moreover, he is to bring the seeds of the tallest plants and all kinds of the most delicious food in order to maintain an ideal condition for existence.

As Yima complies with the detailed instructions of Ahura Mazda, the story suddenly changes texture and takes up an eschatological character. The story states that the stars and the moon and the sun are seen rising and setting once a year. And that the people in the *vara* think a year is only a day. And that every forty years a pair of children, a boy and a girl, are born to each human and animal couple, and those people live the finest lives in the *vara* that Yima made. Then the question is asked, "Who brought the religion of Ahura Mazda into the *vara* that Yima made?" The answer is "the raven." The final question is, "Who is the lord and master in the *vara*?" To this the answer is "Urvatatnara [the son of Zoroaster] and you, Zoroaster!" Here the story not only makes a full circle and returns to Zoroaster, but it also goes a step further to include his son.

The basic structure does seem to parallel both Genesis and Atrahasis, with one important variation.

THE OLD IRANIAN "FLOOD" TALE

A "Introduction and Yima's Kingship"
B "Overpopulation and Expansion of Earth, 1"
C "Overpopulation and Expansion of Earth, 2"
D "Overpopulation and Expansion of Earth, 3"
E "The Great Snow and the Flood from Its Melting"

What is particularly interesting here is that the author seems to have adapted this five-part structure to his own purposes (much as a Hebrew author would have done). Not only does the author have the flood in the last position, but it is unclear whether this flood is something that happened in the past or is going to happen in an eschatological future.

So the parallels observed between Atrahasis and Genesis 1–11 are no longer surprising. We find similar parallels betweeen Atrahasis and other primeval histories. These similar parallels make us feel encouraged that perhaps Genesis 1–11, while drawn from a common stock of tales, was written as a dissent from the civilized pragmatism of the older Atrahasis tradition.

Atrahasis offers population control as the solution to urban overcrowding; Genesis offers dispersion, the nomadic way of life. Population growth is from the very beginning of the Genesis primeval history presented as an unqualified blessing. The blessing of Genesis 1:28 finds a fulfillment in the dispersion "upon the face of the whole earth," which concludes the primeval history. Genesis 1–11 then constitutes a rejection of Babel and Babylon—of civilization itself, if its continuance requires human existence to be treated as a contingent good. For Genesis the existence of a new human was always good.

Of course, what we have observed so far is only suggestive. These parallels, interesting as they are in themselves, only serve to suggest an hypothesis about Genesis 1–11. Genesis 1–11 may have been a considered response to the mythic tradition that survives for us in the Atrahasis epic as well as the Sumerian tradition. We would certainly like to be able to draw conclusions as emphatically as Tigay did from his study of parallels between sections of Atrahasis and the Gilgamesh epic.

> One must rather assume, at the very least, a source common to both texts in which these details had already been brought together. But since most of the common details, as well as the pattern, are most frequently attested as a group in creation literature, to which genre Atrahasis belongs, ultimate inspiration must come from that genre, if not from Atrahasis itself.[22]

Tigay has found far more detailed parallels than we have. Thus, while he can reach an emphatic conclusion, we can only suggest a plausible hypothesis.

Perhaps Genesis 1–11 is written in opposition to the Mesopotamian Atrahasis traditions. Perhaps it argues in favor of the nomadic or pastoral life as a means to unlimited human reproduction. But we need more detailed evidence. If the hypothesis is correct, a detailed examination of Genesis 1–11 in light of Atrahasis should not only reveal previously unobserved connections between the Genesis stories, but also provide solutions to interpretive enigmas within the stories themselves—enigmas which have vexed the ages.

Notes / Chapter II

1. For an earlier version of the argument of this chapter, see Isaac M. Kikawada, "Literary Convention of the Primaeval History," *Annual of Japanese Biblical Institute* 1 (1975):3-21.

2. Richmond Lattimore, trans., *The Iliad of Homer* (Chicago: University of Chicago Press, 1951), bk. 1:1-5.

3. Thomas W. Allen, ed. *Homeri Opera*, v. 5 (Oxford: Oxford University Press, 1919), p. 117. This parallel was first observed in Anne Kilmer, "The Mesopotamian Concept of Overpopulation and its Solution as Reflected in the Mythology," *OR* 41 (1972):16-177. We are also indebted to this article for pointing out the overpopulation motif in Atrahasis, a motif which will be crucial to the entire argument of this chapter.

4. See Hugh Evelyn-White, *Hesiod* (Cambridge, Mass.: Harvard University Press, 1914), p. 497, for the complete quote.

5. Michael N. Nagler, *Spontaneity and Tradition: A Study in Oral Art of Homer* (Berkeley: University of California Press, 1974), pp. 149-50.

6. Tikva Frymer-Kensky, "The Atrahasis Epic and its Significance for Understanding of Genesis 1-9," *Biblical Archeologist* 40 (1977):152. For a useful survey of subsequent interpretations of this command to reproduce, see B. S. Yegerlehner, *Be Fruitful and Multiply* (Diss., Boston University, 1975). David Daube's *The Duty of Procreation* (Edinburgh: Edinburgh University Press, 1982) places this issue in a still broader context.

7. C. A. Benito, *Enki and Ninmah and Enki and the World Order* (Diss., University of Pennsylvania, 1969) is the standard edition and English translation of this text.

8. Kilmer, "Mesopotamian Concept," p. 165.

9. Isaac M. Kikawada, "Two Notes on Eve," *JBL* 91 (1972):33-37.

10. We will be quoting from the definitive edition of W. G. Lambert and A. R. Millard, *Atra-Hasis: The Babylonian Story of the Flood with The Sumerian Flood Story* by Miguel Civil (Oxford: Oxford University Press, 1969) with certain stylistic refinements from the translations of Isaac M. Kikawada, *Literary Conventions Connected with Antediluvian Historiography* (Diss., University of California at Berkeley, 1979). For an alternate reading of the scribe's name, see W. von Soden, "Die erste Tafel des altbabylonischen Atramhasis Mythus," *ZA* 68 (1978):50-94.

11. G. Pettinato, "Die Bestrafung des Menschengeschlects durch die Sintflut," *OR* 47 (1968):165-200. Pettinato suggests that "noise" (*rigmu*) be

interpreted as rebellion, a refusal to do the divinely ordained work. We are following Kilmer, "Mesopotamian Concept," in rejecting this.

12. For a discussion of the relationship between Atrahasis and Enki, see Anne Kilmer, "Speculations on Umul, the First Baby," *AOAT* 25 (1976):265-70.

13. Jørgen Laessøe, "The Atrahasis Epic: A Babylonian History of Mankind," *BOr* 13 (1956):90-102.

14. Lambert and Millard, *Atra-Hasis*, pp. 10-11.

15. Lambert and Millard, pp. 105-15.

16. Kilmer, "Mesopotamian Concept," pp. 160-77.

17. Note the remarks about the demons as means of population control in E. Leichty, "Demons and Population Control," *Expedition* 13 (1971):22-26.

18. The parallels we will be exploring seem to have been first observed in Isaac M. Kikawada, "Literary Convention." Similar, if less detailed, conclusions have been reached by Frymer-Kensky in 1977: "The composer of Genesis 1-9 . . . has used a framework that is at least as old as the epic of Atrahasis, the framework of the Primeval History of Creation-Problem-Flood-Solution, and has retold the story in such a way as to reinterpret an ancient tradition to illuminate fundamental Israelite ideas." Frymer-Kensky, "Atrahasis Epic," p. 154. See also W. M. Clark, "The Flood and the Structure of Pre-Patriarchal History," *ZAW* 81 (1971):186-87, who points in this general direction from within the documentary school.

19. See Lambert and Millard, *Atra-Hasis*, pp. 138-45.

20. Kilmer in her "Speculations on Umul," p. 267, has shown how the Sumerian Flood Story could be combined with the Enki-Ninmah epic to produce a larger epic that would have a similar structure to Atrahasis.

21. The connection was first noted in Kilmer, "Mesopotamian Concept," p. 176. See H. Lommel, "Die Yast's des Awesta," *Quellen der Religionsgeschichte* 15-16 (1927):198-203, and Fritz Wolff, *Die heiligen Bucher der Parsen* (Strassburg: Trubner, 1910). Our translation from the Old Persian is Kikawada's.

22. Jeffrey H. Tigay, *The Evolution of the Gilgamesh Epic* (Philadelphia: University of Pennsylvania Press, 1982), p. 197.

•

Chapter III

Before Abraham Was:
The Unity of Genesis 1–11

1

4:17 Cain knew his wife, and she conceived and bore Enoch; and he built a city, and called the name of the city after the name of his son, Enoch. ¹⁸To Enoch was born Irad; and Irad was the father of Mehujael, and Mehujael the father of Methushael, and Methushael the father of Lamech. ¹⁹And Lamech took two wives; The name of the one was Adah, and the name of the other Zillah. ²⁰Adah bore Jabal; he was the father of those who dwell in tents and have cattle. ²¹His brother's name was Jubal; he was the father of all those who play the lyre and pipe. ²²Zillah bore Tubalcain; he was the forger of all instruments of bronze and iron. The sister of Tubalcain was Naamah.
²³Lamech said to his wives:
"Adah and Zillah, hear my voice;
    you wives of Lamech, hearken to what I say:
I have slain a man for wounding me,
    a young man for striking me.
²⁴If Cain is avenged sevenfold,
    truly Lamech seventy-sevenfold."
²⁵And Adam knew his wife again, and she bore a son and called his name Seth, for she said, "God has appointed for me another child instead of Abel, for Cain slew him." ²⁶To Seth also a son was born, and he called his name Enosh. At that time men began to call upon the name of the Lord.

Few features of Genesis 1–11 seem to the modern reader less intrinsically interesting than the genealogies.¹ And yet this

particular genealogy, which immediately follows the punishment of Cain, contains in microcosm many of the features that we
find distinctive of Genesis 1–11 as a whole.

Remember the general hostility of Genesis primeval history to
civilization, at least according to the interpretation we proposed
in the last chapter. Civilization requires population control, and
thereby regards human life as just a qualified good. How
appropriate then to attribute the origin of the city to the
murderer Cain, and other civilized arts to his descendants. And
lest we think that these descendants might not be as bad as Cain,
the author inserts the taunt of Lamech, who prides himself on
valuing human life even less than Cain. And lest we think that
someone in this family line might be friends with God, there is
inserted the alternative line of Seth, a line which ends not with a
taunt, but rather with men beginning to call upon the Lord.
Presumably civilized men do not.

There is also a nicer point to be observed. Robert Wilson
in his important recent book, *Genealogy and History in the
Biblical World,* has compared this genealogy with other ancient
Near Eastern genealogies and points out that ordinarily the
city builder would be the second on the list, and this builder
would name the city after *his* son.[2] Thus in this Hebrew
genealogy we would expect—and presumably so would a
sophisticated ancient Near Eastern audience—that Enoch would
be the builder and the city would be named after Irad. This
expectation finds a striking, if indirect, confirmation, in that the
first city according to the Mesopotamian tradition is Eridu, as
close to Irad as one can reasonably expect, given the difference in
languages.

Wilson, following Hallo, makes in our opinion the wrong
inference from this fine observation.[3] Wilson and Hallo suggest
that the original genealogy did attribute the first city to Enoch,
and that later editors have added a mistaken gloss, which
accounts for the confusion. However, they admit that no
evidence supports their suggestion, so perhaps we can dare to
suggest a simpler alternative. The author himself was the source
of the manipulation with traditional genealogy, and he
manipulated it in just the same way that he manipulated

primeval history as a whole—namely, against the very civilization that produced it. In keeping with his general interpretation he specifically made the first murderer also the founder of civilization. In other words, as striking as it is for us to have Cain found the first city, it would have been even more striking to an ancient Near Eastern audience familiar with traditional genealogies.

There is one small textual problem with our interpretation of this genealogy as an indictment of civilization. We can understand why Jubal and Tubalcain were descended from Cain, for they were the first musician and metal worker respectively. These were specialized occupations associated with civilization. But why is Jabal descended from Cain? "Those who dwell in tents and have cattle" are presumably the shepherds, the pastoral peoples who live outside civilization and in whose name the author of Genesis seems to be condemning civilization itself.

Unlike the documentary analyst, we cannot invoke a napping editor to remove an unpleasant inconsistency. This may be a small textual problem of a single phrase in a single verse, but given the high literary standards which we expect Genesis to meet this is an extremely important difficulty. Let us look at the text more closely. At first glance Jabal whose descendants dwelt in tents and had cattle seems to be out of place among these civilized firsts. Jabal's descendants were not the first shepherds (Abel had flocks), and shepherding itself is not a consequence of civilization but rather an antecedent. However, our problem derives not from the Hebrew text, but rather from the usual English translation. The word usually translated as "cattle" is *miqnēh*. Actually it means possessions, particularly animate possessions, such as cattle. *Miqnēh* is derived from the verb *qānāh*, to buy or possess. Hence the unrecognized Joseph will hear his brothers plead, "Buy (*qānāh*) us and our land for food, and we with our land will be slaves to Pharaoh." In other words, *miqnēh* means a living possession with the added connotation that the possessor has legal title as he would for something commercially bought. (The feminine form of *miqnēh* actually can mean purchase price.) *Miqnēh* might refer to cattle, but cattle legally owned. Therefore, when God creates "cattle," when he gives Adam dominion over the "cattle," when Adam names them, when Abel tends his "flocks," *miqnēh* is not the word used, for these herds have nothing to do with legal transactions. *Miqnēh* is used only after the beginning of civilization; verse 4:20 is its first appearance. And so the word is perhaps better translated by the general term *livestock,* which in English still retains a slight connotation of animals owned in legal terms and for commercial purposes. Nonetheless, even this translation may be too narrow in the kinds of living possessions it suggests to a modern reader. This is shown the next time *miqnēh* appears, Genesis 13:2. "Now Abram was very rich in *miqnēh,* in silver, and in gold." The gold and silver constituted Abram's inanimate wealth; *miqnēh* his animate wealth. He had accumulated this wealth by allowing the pharaoh to take Sarai into his harem. Abram's profits during this stay are listed, and constitute what eventually will be summarized as his *miqnēh:* "sheep, oxen, he-asses, menservants, female servants, she-asses, and camels." Among your *miqnēh* can be numbered your slaves. The language of Genesis permits both cattle barons and slave traders to claim descent from Cain through Jubal. Perhaps the sons of Jubal did discover, long before Abram visited Egypt, that the civilized profession most profitable is the flesh trade.

To summarize, the genealogy of Genesis 4:17-26 is an indictment of civilization, an indictment that associates civilization with a murderous disregard for human life. The full rhetorical effect of this indictment depends upon familiarity with contrary ancient Near Eastern literary traditions. And the subtlety of this indictment is revealed in the very wording of the single phrase in the received text that at first glance seems to weigh decisively against our interpretation.

Ironically, this very genealogy has frequently been used as evidence in favor of the documentary hypothesis. Specifically, the comparison of it with the genealogy that immediately follows in chapter 5 has revealed contradictions between the two that seem to make a unitary reading impossible. In the following diagram (based on Wilson), the apparent contradictions are indicated by the dotted lines.[4]

57

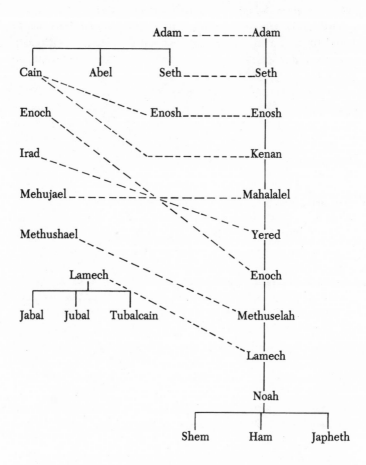

The documentary approach resolves these contradictions easily enough by attributing the two genealogies to two different traditions. The first genealogy, which traces the spread of sin, originates in the same tradition as the Adam and Eve and Cain and Abel stories, and hence is to be attributed to the Yahwist. The second genealogy, in contrast, traces the transmission of the image of God from Adam all the way to Noah, who is going to preserve it from the flood. This derives from the same tradition as the creation story of Genesis 1 and hence is to be attributed to the Priestly source.

Of course, this documentary approach only postpones our confrontation with these inconsistencies between the two genealogies. When we ask why the editor was not concerned enough to remove the inconsistencies, we are told that the editor was not bothered by such things. We can, of course, then ask why, if ancient Near Eastern editors were not bothered by such inconsistent genealogies, should we assume that ancient Near Eastern authors were. Perhaps it is our notion of "inconsistency" that is out of place here. Wilson in his systematic study thinks that indeed this may well be the case; he in particular does not think that we need to attribute these two genealogies to different sources.

> We noted that in societies that use oral genealogies, the form of a genealogy frequently changes when its function changes. Thus, in a given society at a particular time there may be several apparently contradictory versions of the same genealogy. These versions are not viewed as contradictory by the people who use them, however, for the people know that each version is correct in the particular context in which it is cited. The "contradiction" is apparent only to someone who is not familiar with the way in which genealogies are created and used. A similar view of the nature of genealogy may have been in the mind of the Priestly Writer, and if this was the case, he would not have been disturbed by the "contradictions" between Gen. 4 and 5, for he would have recognized that each genealogy has a different function and that the form of each is appropriate to that function.[5]

Wilson is an ideal witness for us not only because he has made a more thorough study of ancient Near Eastern genealogies than anyone else, but also because, as his last sentence shows, he himself supports the documentary hypothesis. He supports the documentary hypothesis, but he just does not think that the genealogies of Genesis 4–5 provide any decisive evidence in its favor.

But what of the function of all the genealogies in Genesis 1–11 as a whole? There are four indisputable genealogies within it, the two we have discussed above (4:7-26; 5:1-32) and the genealogies on each side of the Babel story (10:1-32; 11:10-32). Moreover, there are two other passages that could be considered as broadly genealogical. Genesis 2:4 reads: "These are the generations of the heavens and the earth when they were created." The word *generations (tôlᵉdôt)* is the same as would be used in a genealogy. We might then consider this verse not as the conclusion to the creation story, but as an independent transitional unit floating between it and the Garden of Eden story. If that is the case, we would expect a similar connective passage between the Garden of Eden story and that of Cain and Abel. This would have to be Genesis 4:1-2: "Now Adam knew Eve his wife, and she conceived and bore Cain, saying 'I have gotten a man with the help of the Lord.' And again, she bore his brother Abel." We have here the substance of a short genealogy without the distinctive vocabulary, much as in Genesis 2:4 we have the form without the normal content. Between the Cain and Abel story and that of Noah, and between Noah and Babel, and between Babel and Abraham we have the form and content together. In short, if we take 2:4 and 4:1-2 as proto-genealogies, then the genealogical material can be seen as simply reinforcing the general structure, as the following chart makes clear.[6]

GENESIS 1–11

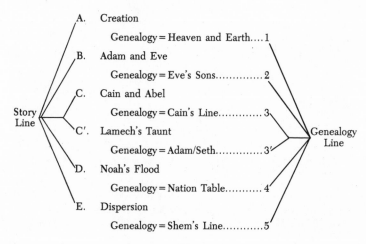

Thus, while the genealogies may well serve to strengthen the structure of the Genesis primeval history, they are also interludes between the stories, interludes that give actual substance to the blessing/command of 1:28—"Be fruitful and multiply, and fill the earth." The "begats" embody the blessing.

The Hebrew author knew that civilized Near Easterners did not regard a birth as necessarily a blessing. He was perhaps having some fun with this when he made all of these civilizations descended from Noah through his bad son Ham. The very civilizations, which bemoaned overpopulation in their myths, had as their common progenitor the same Ham who was so proud of having seen his father's nakedness.

The genealogy from Noah is also interesting on formal grounds. While the genealogies from Cain and Seth were linear in the sense that they only recorded the names of eldest sons, this one is segmented, a real genealogical tree that records all sons. Why the change? It would be tempting to think that this fuller genealogy is meant to signify a historiographical watershed (if you will pardon the expression). After the flood we could keep track of all lines and should because many of them will reach down into the present.

If the Hebrew author was using genealogical form as an indicator of the discontinuity between antediluvian and post-diluvian times, he was being original, at least for an ancient Near Eastern author. A parallel can be found in the Sanskrit flood story; in this story a linear genealogy leads to Manu Vaivasvata, the Sanskrit Noah, and a segmented genealogy is recorded from him.[7]

We should not make too much of this, however. Look, for instance, at the last genealogy of Genesis 1–11, after the Tower of Babel. It begins:

> 11:10 These are the descendants of Shem. When Shem was a hundred years old, he became the father of Arpachshad two years after the flood; [11]and Shem lived after the birth of Arpachshad five hundred years, and had other sons and daughters.
> [12]When Arpachshad had lived thirty-five years, he became the father of Shelah; [13]and Arpachshad lived after the birth of Shelah four hundred and three years, and had other sons and daughters.
> [14]When Shelah had lived thirty years, he became the father of

Eber; [15]and Shelah lived after the birth of Eber four hundred and three years, and had other sons and daughters.

We have already seen the way in which the genealogy of Genesis 4–5 combines the form and content of the two proto-genealogies: the form of Genesis 2:4 and the content of 4:1-2. Now we have another synthesis. The Seth and Cain genealogies were linear; the Noah genealogies were segmented; but this last genealogy is both and neither, in that it mentions other than first sons but does not mention them by name. We can now see that of the three genealogies—or of the five, if we count the first two—all are given in different forms. In what to our eyes is a most unpromising genre, the author of Genesis 1–11 (if there was only one) still found a way to exhibit his literary dexterity. Apparently he invites us to take delight in his ability to create variety for its own sake. The substance of the genealogy details how man in imitation of God was being fruitful and multiplying. Our author, the genealoger, seems himself to have been obeying this command at the formal, literary level.

He is doing this in the genealogies between the stories. And perhaps he is doing it in the forms of divine address within the stories themselves. He there seems to vary divine address for its own sake. In the creation story God is Elohim; in Adam and Eve he is usually Yahweh Elohim (something documentary critics fail to emphasize); in Cain and Abel he is simply Yahweh; in Noah sometimes Elohim, sometimes Yahweh; by the Tower of Babel the author has exhausted all the possibilities, and in that brief story returns quietly to Yahweh, the most important form of address. There may be simple matters of decorum or profound truths of theology governing the use of divine names elsewhere in the Pentateuch; in Genesis 1–11, however, the inherited divine names, like the genealogies, are varied for variety's sake. Man, God's image and likeness, should sense God's pleasure in his creative fecundity.

2

We suggested in the last chapter that Genesis 1–11 shares structural features with the old Babylonian history of Atrahasis. A distinctive feature of this structure is that the middle three episodes are repetitive. Episode 1 is a creation; episode 5 is a resolution; but episodes 2-4 are three threats to mankind. Their repetitive character is fairly obvious in Atrahasis, but not so obvious in Genesis.

If the author of Genesis 1-11 was thinking in terms of this older primeval historiographic structure, then we would expect a closer examination of the Adam and Eve, Cain and Abel, and Noah and the flood stories to reveal significant similarities. Moreover, if he was as skillful in putting together these episodes as he was in exploiting the relatively unpromising form of genealogy, then we would expect more than repetition. We would expect him to find a way to repeat with sufficient variations to give a real sense of movement and progression. To expect both repetition and progression is no small order, but we believe this is exactly what we find.

To start with, these three central stories have essentially the same plot. The numerous parallels in plot are best shown in a synoptic chart. (See pages 64-66.)

In short, the plots of these three stories are essentially the same. Each has an introductory section in which origins are accounted for and a peaceful setting described. Each then tells of a wicked action to which God reacts unfavorably, and this reaction itself provokes a human response. Finally, each story recounts a divine curse, followed by a threefold mitigation of that curse. The stories are repetitive, but in what way can the three taken together be said to progress?

Let us look at the three stories in purely quantitative terms. We have seen that they share a roughly tripartite structure: introduction, action, result. While the plots are much the same in general terms, the quantitative distribution of each story between these three parts is very different. The introductory sections are twenty-one verses or two hundred eighty-one Hebrew words for Adam and Eve, two verses or twenty-eight words for Cain and Abel, and one verse or eleven words for Noah. In proportional terms, the introduction is approximately one-half of the story of Adam and Eve, only one-eighth of the story of Cain and Abel, and merely one-ninety-sixth of the Noah story. Thus, when the three stories are examined synoptically,

SYNOPSIS OF ADAM, CAIN, AND NOAH STORIES

Adam and Eve	Cain and Abel	Noah's Flood
A. Origin of human (*'ādām*) principals accounted for:		
1. Origin of mankind *'ādām* and plants created 2:5-14	Origin of 2nd generation Children of *hā'ādām* 4:1-2	Origin of the multitude *hā'ādām* began to multiply 6:1
2. Animals and Eve created 2:15-25		
B. Peaceful setting on the *ground: 'adāmāh*:		
1. There was not a man to till *hā'adāmāh* 2:5	Tiller of *'adāmāh* Shepherd of flock 4:2	Upon the face of *hā'adāmāh* Daughters were born 6:1
2. To till *hā'adāmāh* in the garden 2:15		

I

Adam and Eve	Cain and Abel	Noah's Flood
C. Trigger action: Eating of the tree after woman *saw how good.* 3:6	1. Offering of fruit of the ground by Cain. 4:3 2. Murder of Abel his brother by Cain. 4:8	Sons of God *saw* daughters *how good* and married and had children. 6:2-4
II D. YHWH's unfavorable reaction: "What is this that you have done?" 3:9	1. He did not gaze upon the offering of Cain. 4:5 2. "Where is Abel your brother?" 4:9	YHWH was sorry . . . "I will blot out man." 6:5-7
E. Human Counter-reaction: "The woman whom you gave me, she gave me fruit . . . and I ate." 3:12	1. Cain became angry, his face fell. 4:5 2. "Am I my brother's keeper?" 4:9	Earth being destroyed and filled with violence 6:11-13

(Continued on next page)

Adam and Eve	Cain and Abel	Noah's Flood
F. "Curse involving the ground (*adāmāh*) pronounced by YHWH: "Cursed: *arûrāh* is the ground because of you." 3:17	"Cursed: *arûr* are you more than the ground." 4:11	1. Never again to *curse*: $l^e qallel$ the ground. 8:21 2. Noah—*cursed*: *arûr* are you (Canaan). 9:25
III. G. Threefold mitigation/protection: Leather clothing Banishment Guarding of the tree of life 3:21-24	Vengeance Sign of protection Wandering and Nod (city of refuge) 4:15-16	1. Not curse again Not to smite again Not to cease 8:21-22 2. Blessing, "Be fruitful . . ." Food—animals and plants Scattering of people 9:8-19

we learn that the introductory part of the stories diminishes proportionally in three steps. Further, note that in the Adam and Eve story, the creation of Adam and the creation of Eve are narrated in two parallel but separate stages—the first being the creation of Adam and the plants, the second the creation of animals and woman. These two together constitute the introduction, making the Adam and Eve story quite top-heavy.

As for the action part of the stories, the Adam and Eve story narrates this in thirteen verses or one-fourth of the story. In contrast, the Cain and Abel story has a double middle—"the Offerings" and "the Murder"—that takes up more than one-half of the story, or ten verses. Moreover, the sequence of "trigger action-divine reaction-human counter-reaction" is repeated twice in these two episodes. This makes the Cain and Abel story middle-heavy.

In contrast, in the story of Noah's flood, this middle sequence is summarily told in twelve verses, which constitute less than one-eighth of the story. More than 80 percent of the flood story is given to the narration of the actualized curse of the ground and of the protection of human beings and other species of animals. In the main, the narrative of Noah's flood is a curse story, a point made clear when Yahweh smells the sweet smell of the postdiluvian sacrifice and says: "I will never again curse the ground because of man . . . neither will I ever again destroy every living creature as I have done" (8:21). Furthermore, the curse idea is taken up on the human scale in the last episode of the story, when Noah curses Canaan. As the Adam and Eve story has a double introduction, and as Cain and Abel have a double middle action, so the flood story has a double curse—the curse of Yahweh and the curse of Noah.

To summarize, when the stories of Adam and Eve, Cain and Abel, and Noah's flood are viewed quantitatively, we notice that the greatest portion of the narrative is spent for the stage setting part of the story in the Adam and Eve story; the greatest portion of the narrative of Cain and Abel is reserved for the middle of the story; then, in the Noah narrative, we find the conclusion of the story becoming the story in itself and all of the other parts being reduced to a brief prelude. So the interrelationship among these three stories reflects a progressive dramatic development in three stages that can be observed even quantitatively.

But do these enigmatic stories themselves bear on the themes we have considered central to Genesis 1–11? What, to take the least promising case, does the Adam and Eve story have to say about reproduction and the nomadic way of life? Once we ask this question many of the enigmas that have long troubled interpreters of this story suddenly dissolve.

The story shows how God tried the sedentary life for man, and it did not work. Adam and Eve were given a garden to keep. They could live off their plants. The garden, significantly, was watered by rivers clearly associated with the great centers of ancient civilizations.[8] For instance, there is the Euphrates "which flows east of Assyria." Agriculture, unlike herding, provides the basis for civilization. And Eve wants to be wise. Wisdom—that highest product of civilization?—is somehow associated with the central tree in the garden. Civilization is the fruit of agriculture most beautiful to look at.

And yet what happens when Adam and Eve try to become civilized? They become ashamed of their genitals. What does this shame signify? Perhaps that they no longer want to fulfill God's command to be fruitful and multiply.[9] And if they manage to become immortal, they will still be able to resist this command. God, of course, is fully equal to the situation. God's curses on them associate procreation with the nomadic life. He curses the ground for Adam—when Cain is later cursed from the ground, he is supposed to become a wanderer for the rest of his life.[10] God specifies that Adam shall eat plants of the field, perhaps in contrast to cultivated plants of the garden. Certainly God replaces the apron of fig leaves with garments of skins—that is, replaces the clothes of tillers with the clothes of herders. If Adam tries to cultivate, he will have not figs, but thorns and thistles.

Since Eve was trying to avoid reproduction, her punishment is associated with it. She will be greatly pained precisely in the act of bearing fruit. After the curse, Adam is perhaps making an act of submission when he finally names his wife. He has named all the animals, but he is only now getting around to his own helpmate. Now we know what she is to help him with. "The man called his wife's name Eve, because she was mother of all living."[11] And we might hear bitterness when Eve herself says, "I have gotten a man with the help of the Lord." The help of the Lord was the expulsion from the Garden. And this first fruit of her womb is bitter, for it is Cain, who attempts to return to the sedentary, agricultural way of life but is rejected by God.

"Why are you angry, and why has your countenance fallen? If you do well, will you not be accepted? And if you do not do well, sin is couching at the door."[12] Sin is always couching at doors, all doors.

3

If Genesis 1-11 does follow the Atrahasis pattern, we would not only expect the three central episodes to be repetitive but also episode one (creation) and episode 5 (resolution) to be tied together. We would expect to find features shared by these two stories, perhaps features not found in the central three episodes. (Of course, the documentary hypothesis predicts differently, for the creation story and Tower of Babel are attributed to the Priestly and Yahwist sources respectively.)

There are a number of parallels between these two stories not shared by the central three. In both, no human principal is mentioned by name. *Adām* is used in the general sense of mankind. *Šāmayim* for "sky" is used in both stories. In both stories, God uses the plural verb in cohortative: "Let us make man" in Genesis 1:26 parallels "Let us go down, and there confuse" of Genesis 11:6. More important than any of these particular verbal observations (and at least one of them is disputable) is the general point that the Tower of Babel story does tell of the fulfillment of the creation story. Genesis 1:28 has the blessing/command, "Be fruitful and multiply, and fill the earth," whereas the Tower of Babel story tells of the dispersion that is the means of realizing this blessing/command concretely.

These points, especially the last, are suggestive. And if we had been claiming that Genesis 1-11 was just an interesting *collection* of stories, this would be enough perhaps to establish a loose pattern. We have been arguing, however, that Genesis 1-11 is an extraordinary literary achievement unified with consummate subtlety and skill. To such high claims two objections are scarcely avoidable.

First, while the Tower of Babel story is thematically appropriate, it is too slight a literary effort to be anything but anticlimactic for the drama that began with the creation of the world. Second, while Genesis 1:28 does indeed announce a theme relevant to the conclusion of Genesis 1–11, it is hardly the center of the magisterial creation account. This blessing is not unimportant, but we can hardly say that it governs the whole of the creation account, as it should if the creation is only a prologue to what comes after (and not an autonomous work as the documentary analysis suggests). These are both important and legitimate objections, which will have to be answered with care.[13]

What does it mean to say that the Tower of Babel is an inappropriate conclusion to Genesis 1–11? Surely, this cannot mean that Babel is simply too short. Let us suppose that the author of Genesis 1–11 is also the author of the rest of Genesis as well. Or, to be less ambitious, let us suppose that he composed Genesis 1–11 as the initial section of an already existent series of patriarchical narratives. Our author would in either of these cases want a final episode that would propel us into the patriarchical history. We go through the Tower of Babel story rather quickly, and it ends with a general dispersion. And before we know it we are into the Abraham story, which begins with the dispersion of Abram himself out of Mesopotamia. So we can well understand why the author of Genesis 1–11 might have chosen to make the last story of his primeval history the shortest; thematically it might be a conclusion, but rhetorically it was a transition to the main subject of his work.

Nonetheless, whatever the relationship of the Tower of Babel story to what follows, and however brief it is, we should still expect it to fulfill the high literary standards of what has gone before. In that sense it must not be anticlimactic. Let us look at the story closely.

11:1 Now the whole earth had one language and few words. ²And as men migrated from the east, they found a plain in the land of Shinar and settled there. ³And they said to one another, "Come, let us make bricks, and burn them thoroughly." And they had brick for stone, and bitumen for mortar. ⁴Then they said, "Come, let us build ourselves a city, and a tower with its top in the heavens, and let us make a name for ourselves, lest we be scattered abroad upon the face of the whole earth." ⁵And the Lord came down to see the city and the tower, which the sons of men had built. ⁶And the Lord said, "Behold, they are one people, and they have all one language; and this is only the beginning of what they will do; and nothing that they propose to do will now be impossible for them. ⁷Come, let us go down, and there confuse their language, that they may not understand one another's speech." ⁸So the Lord scattered them abroad from there over the face of all the earth, and they left off building the city. ⁹Therefore its name was called Babel, because there the Lord confused the language of all the earth; and from there the Lord scattered them abroad over the face of all the earth.

A reading of the story shows the justness of Cassuto's complaint that this is not strictly a story about the tower.

> Although the construction of the tower occupies an important place in the narrative, it is not the main subject. The principal theme is the dispersion of mankind over the face of the whole earth, a matter that God purposed and that was ultimately fulfilled in accordance with the Divine will, notwithstanding human attempts to obstruct it. The tower is only a detail in the episode—part of the gigantic city that men sought to build in order to achieve their goal. Not without reason, therefore, does the end of the story refer only to the suspension of the building of the city but not of the construction of the tower (v.8: *and they left off building the city*).[14]

Cassuto quite rightly argues that the traditional Jewish designation of this story—"The Generation of Division"—fits it far better than "The Tower of Babel." This contention points to another parallel between the creation account of Genesis 1–2 and this story. Babel tells of the generation of human division; the creation account tells how God on the first three days created the cosmic divisions. Genesis 1–2:3 tells how the cosmic divisions found their fulfillment in God's command to man to be fruitful, multiply, and fill the earth. Genesis 11 tells why God decided that to make men obey his command, he had to create divisions within them.

There is a wonderful irony in the story's conclusion. It is not just a story about "them," about the Babylonians. It is a story that covers the Hebrew author and his hearers. After all, their language is no longer the same as that of the Tigris and Euphrates. Hebrew is now a separate tongue. The ideas might be intelligible across the linguistic frontier (as they would be in wisdom literature), but the physical sounds of the languages are mutually unintelligible. It is a master stroke, therefore, that this story more than any other in the primeval history plays with the sounds of Hebrew.

Cassuto observes that the story is dominated by the sounds "b," "l," "n."

> In v. 3: *hābhā nilbᵉnā´ lᵉbhēnīm* ["Come, let us make bricks]; and thereafter, *ibid. lāhem hallᵉbhēnā lᵉ·abhen* ["they had brick for stone"]; v. 4: *hābhā nibhne lānū* ["Come, let us build ourselves"]; v. 5: *bānū bᵉnē* ["the sons (of men) had built"]; v. 7: *wᵉnābhᵉlā* ["let us confuse"]; v. 8: *wayyahᵈᵉlū libhnōth* ["and they left off building"]; v. 9: *Bābhel* ["Babel," "Babylon"] *bālal* ["confused"].[15]

This resonating play with sounds is only the beginning of the linguistic complexity of this story. It takes Cassuto a full two pages just to enumerate all the other examples of word play in this brief story: alliterations, paranomasias, puns, and the like. The story about the Lord confusing human language into diversity is written in a style that is brilliantly untranslatable. A Hebrew could not help but be amused at the sly skill with which what is incomprehensible to the rest of the world is made comprehensible to its own audience, how a language in its very particularity and isolation from others can be made to say more than it says.

Nonetheless, even a reader without Hebrew can appreciate the intricate architecture of the story, an architecture that even a Babylonian ziggurat builder would have to admire. At the most obvious level the story divides itself into two parallel episodes: man's civilizing sin and God's humbling response.

11:1 Now the whole earth had one language and few words. ²And as men migrated from the east, they found a plain in the land of Shinar and settled there. ³And they said to one another,

⁶And the Lord said, "Behold, they are one people, and they have all one language; and this is only the beginning of what they will do; and nothing that they propose to do will now be

72

"Come, let us make bricks, and burn them thoroughly." And they had brick for stone, and bitumen for mortar. ⁴Then they said, "Come, let us build ourselves a city, and a tower with its top in the heavens, and let us make a name for ourselves, lest we be scattered abroad upon the face of the whole earth." ⁵And the Lord came down to see the city and the tower, which the sons of men had built. impossible for them. ⁷Come, let us go down, and there confuse their language, that they may not understand one another's speech." ⁸So the Lord scattered them abroad from there over the face of all the earth, and they left off building the city. ⁹Therefore its name was called Babel, because there the Lord confused the language of all the earth; and from there the Lord scattered them abroad over the face of all the earth.

The parallels between the first and second columns are obvious enough. The earth has one language; God beholds the one language. Men say "let us build up"; God says "let us go down."[16] Men worry about being scattered; God scatters them. Men want to make a name for themselves; God gives the name *Babel*. God comes down from heaven to see the city and tower; men go out from the city to all the world.

Fokkelman, while seeing the close verbal parallels between these two parts, argues that at a deeper level the story is chiastically structured. He summarizes the story as follows:

The unity of language (A) and of place (B) and intensive communication (C) induce the men to plans and inventions (D), especially to building (E) a city and a tower (F). God's intervention is the turning-point (X). He watches the buildings (F') people make (E') and launches a counter-plan (D') because of which communication becomes impossible (C') and the unity of place (B') and of language (A') is broken.[17]

Radday, a few years before, had suggested a simpler chiastic arrangement. However much we might disagree with this or that point in Fokkelman, Radday's analysis is at least unobjectionable.[18]

    a   human unity (vs. 1-2)
      b   man speaks and acts (vs. 3-4)
        c   God comes down to see (v. 5)
      b   God speaks and acts (vs. 6-7)
    a   human dispersion (vs. 8-9)

Whether we accept Radday's analysis or the more detailed one of Fokkelman, it is clear that the author of this little story has managed to combine a chiastic structure with a simple repetitive structure. This structure is entirely in keeping with the author's shown skill in using repetitions in the three previous stories and the way he exploited genealogies. The author's skill is also reflected by the extraordinary and entirely appropriate word play that dominates the style of this story, and the way this story subtly reflects the original creation. Certainly the Tower of Babel—or, if you prefer, the Generation of Human Divisions—is a worthy conclusion to the Genesis primeval history.

4

The Tower of Babel story is a suitable conclusion to the Genesis primeval history. The question remains whether or not the magisterial creation account is an appropriate introduction. Remember, we are not here questioning its literary worthiness as we did the Tower of Babel story. We are instead concerned about its thematic connection with the Tower of Babel.[19]

PROLOGUE

1:1 In the beginning God created the heavens and the earth. [2]The earth was without form and void, and darkness was upon the face of the deep; and the Spirit of God was moving over the face of the waters.

DAY 1

3 And God said, "Let there be light"; and there was light. [4]And God saw that the light was good; and God separated

DAY 4

14 And God said, "Let there be lights in the firmament of the heavens to separate the day from the night; and let them

the light from the darkness. [5]God called the light Day, and the darkness he called Night. And there was evening and there was morning, one day.

DAY 2

6 And God said, "Let there be a firmament in the midst of the waters, and let it separate the waters from the waters." [7]And God made the firmament and separated the waters which were under the firmament from the waters which were above the firmament. And it was so.

be for signs and for seasons and for days and years, [15]and let there be lights in the firmament of the heavens to give light upon the earth." And it was so. [16]And God made the two great lights, the greater light to rule the day, and the lesser light to rule the night; he made the stars also. [17]And God set them in the firmament of the heavens to give light upon the earth, [18]and to rule over the day and over the night, and to separate the light from the darkness. And God saw that it was good. [19]And there was evening and there was morning, a fourth day.

DAY 5

20 And God said, "Let the waters bring forth swarms of living creatures, and let birds fly above the earth across the firmament of the heavens." [21]So God created the great sea monsters and every living creature that moves, with which the waters swarm, according to their

⁸And God called the firmament Heaven. And there was evening and there was morning, a second day.

kinds, and every winged bird according to its kind. And God saw that it was good. ²²And God blessed them, saying, "Be fruitful and multiply and fill the waters in the seas, and let birds multiply on the earth." ²³And there was evening and there was morning, a fifth day.

DAY 3

9 And God said, "Let the waters under the heavens be gathered together into one place, and let the dry land appear." And it was so. ¹⁰God called the dry land Earth, and the waters that were gathered together he called Seas. And God saw that it was good. ¹¹And God said, "Let the earth put forth vegetation, plants yielding seed, and fruit trees bearing fruit in which is their seed, each according to its kind, upon the earth." And it was so. ¹²The earth brought forth vegetation, plants yielding seed according to their own kinds, and trees bearing fruit in

DAY 6

24 And God said, "Let the earth bring forth living creatures according to their kinds: cattle and creeping things and beasts of the earth according to their kinds." And it was so. ²⁵And God made the beasts of the earth according to their kinds and the cattle according to their kinds, and everything that creeps upon the ground according to its kind. And God saw that it was good.

²⁶Then God said, "Let us make man in our image, after our likeness; and let them have dominion over the fish of the sea, and over the birds of the air, and over the cattle, and

which is their seed, each according to its kind. And God saw that it was good. [13]And there was evening and there was morning, a third day.

over all the earth, and over every creeping thing that creeps upon the earth." [27]So God created man in his own image, in the image of God he created him; male and female he created them. [28]And God blessed them, and God said to them, "Be fruitful and multiply, and fill the earth and subdue it; and have dominion over the fish of the sea and over the birds of the air and over every living thing that moves upon the earth." [29]And God said, "Behold, I have given you every plant yielding seed which is upon the face of all the earth, and every tree with seed in its fruit; you shall have them for food. [30]And to every beast of the earth, and to every bird of the air, and to everything that creeps on the earth, everything that has the breath of life, I have given every green plant for food." And it was so. [31]And God saw everything that he had made, and behold, it was very good. And there was evening and

there was morning,
a sixth day.

DAY 7
(EPILOGUE)

2:1 Thus the heavens and the earth were finished, and all the host of them. [2]And on the seventh day God finished his work which he had done, and he rested on the seventh day from all his work which he had done. [3]So God blessed the seventh day and hallowed it, because on it God rested from all his work which he had done in creation.

This way of printing the account helps answer one of the perennial questions: why the sun, moon, and stars are created three days after the light. Clearly the creation account is organized in two parallel groups of three. In the first group, regions are created: night and day, firmament (and atmosphere) and oceans, the earth. In the second group, the corresponding inhabitants of these regions are created: astronomical bodies, birds and fish, land animals and man. This, however, raises another perennial question: why are the plants created on day three rather than on day six? The plants, we would think, should be grouped with the living beings rather than the earth. What classification criterion was the author using that put the plants even before the sun?

We think that a clue to this comes from the peculiar description of the animals of dry land, "cattle and creeping things and beasts of the earth."[20] We can say that this phrase is intended as a synecdoche for all living land animals, but why select these as representatives? "Beasts of the earth" could refer to all land animals. Why then include cattle and the creepers? At first this does not seem to be much of a clue. As commonly happens with this creation account, the attempt to explain one incongruity simply leads us to another. Yet look at the way the author summarizes this list of earth animals in 1:28: "every living thing that moves upon the earth."

The author is preoccupied with locomotion. He puts the birds in day five because they move in the air "across the firmament of the heavens." If we classify animals according to locomotion, then those animals that move on the earth can be subclassified into three types. There are cattle and the like which walk on top of it; there are the creepers and crawlers which slide along it; and finally there are "beasts of the earth" which dig through it. (Remember, by the way, that the punishment of the serpent has to do with its manner of locomotion.)

Once we see this, then the reason the plants are consigned to day three is obvious. They, unlike the birds of the air, the fishes of the sea, the animals of the earth, *and* astronomical bodies, lack the capacity for locomotion. In that sense they are places, rather than living beings.[21]

Nonetheless, the author certainly recognizes that plants have something in common with the beings of days five and six, something which the astronomical bodies of day four lack. The plants yield "seed according to their own kind," much as the birds, fish, and land animals bring forth progeny according to their own kind. Hence we can see that days three and four are, in a sense, a transition between the inanimate creation of days one and two and the fully animate creation of days five and six. To be fully alive one must have capacity for both locomotion and reproduction.

Note the author is careful to make sure that God himself is fully alive according to the terms of the creation account itself. We first encounter God in motion; his Spirit is moving across the face of the deep. The whole of the creation account can be read as the result of this motion. And the creative motion of God has as its highest product his reproduction of himself according to his own kind—or at least the closest he can come to that, a creature in his own image and likeness.

79

This creature he bids to be worthy of his creator. "Be fruitful and multiply, and fill the earth and subdue it." Mankind, to live fully, to be the image and likeness of God, must exercise his dual capacities (a duality emphasized by the doubling "image and likeness"). He must both reproduce and move. Yet these two capacities are really intimately connected, as the Tower of Babel story shows. If he is to reproduce to his fullest, he must be willing to give up his sedentary way of life, much as Abram will be called to, much as Moses will call the Hebrew people to.

To be sure, there will be a Sabbath, moments of rest in this effort to have dominion over the earth. These will be kept because God himself rested after creation was finished. And yet this short period of rest will only serve to remind that man's role is far from finished.

Atrahasis argues in the name of the gods (the nonreproducing astronomical bodies?) that mankind should curb its reproductive drive, and thus concede that human existence is a conditional good. The Hebrew author responds that procreation is God's greatest command to us, our greatest blessing. What about overpopulation? To this civilized question the Hebrew gives a nomadic reply.

Our vitality is based on two powers, our power to reproduce and our power to move. In this good universe, this divinely ordained world, to fulfill one of these capacities requires that we fulfill the other. To have progeny as numerous as the sands we must be willing to move over those sands as the spirit of God once moved over the face of the waters.

Notes / Chapter III

1. Robert Wilson, *Genealogy and History in the Biblical World* (New Haven: Yale University Press, 1977) is a significant attempt to make them less so.
2. Wilson, pp. 13-58.
3. W. W. Hallo, "Antediluvian Cities," *JCS* 23 (1971):57-67.
4. Wilson, p. 161.
5. Wilson, p. 166.
6. The chart is based on Claus Westermann, *Genesis 1–11* (Neukirche: 1966), pp. 2-24.
7. Wendy O'Flaherty, *Hindu Myths* (Harmondsworth, England: Penguin, 1975).
8. Speiser sensibly concludes his own study of the Rivers of Paradise: "The biblical text, the traditions of ancient Mesopotamia, the geographic history of the

land at the head of the Persian Gulf, and the surviving building practices in that marshy country point jointly to an older garden land, richly watered, and favored by religion and literature alike—the kind of Paradise, in short, that local tradition still locates at the confluence of the Euphrates and the Tigris." E. A. Speiser, *Oriental and Biblical Studies* (Philadelphia: University of Pennsylvania Press, 1967), p. 34.

9. This helps explain the quandary many interpreters have found themselves in when attempting to explain the "original sin." They have sensed (correctly) that the sin had to do with sexual intercourse. But they have never been able to respond effectively to skeptics who find no evidence of intercourse and therefore prefer to interpret "knowledge" more inclusively. (For a convenient survey, see John A. Bailey, "Initiation and the Primal Woman in Genesis 2-3," *JBL* 89 (1970):137-50). Both sides have part of the answer. The sin was sexual, but was both a sin of omission and a sin that was the result of having knowledge in the inclusive sense. And hence we can agree with the general conclusion of J. L. McKenzie decades ago that the ancient Hebrews would have understood the Garden of Eden as a story about "the perversion of sexual life from its primitive integrity." J. L. McKenzie, "The Literary Characteristics of Genesis 2-3," *Theological Studies* 15 (1954):571.

10. "Cursed from the ground" could also be translated "more cursed than the ground"—and such a translation would tie the Cain curse even more closely to the earlier curse of Adam. We are indebted for this suggestion to Jo Milgrom.

11. Isaac M. Kikawada, in his "Two Notes on Eve," *JBL* 91 (1972):33-37, explores two parallels between this passage and the description of Mami in the Atrahasis epic. He also suggests that "I have gotten a man" might be better translated "I have *created* a man."

12. For a discussion of textual difficulties in this divine speech, see G. R. Castellino, "Genesis IV, 7," *VT* 10 (1960):442-45.

13. W. M. Clark, "The Flood and the Structure of Pre-patriarchal History," *ZAW* 81 (1971):206, has decisively refuted one attempt to make the Tower of Babel story an appropriate conclusion to what has gone before: "The pattern of ever increasing sin reaching a culmination in the Babel incident is not convincing. The scattering of mankind is not as severe or universal punishment as the flood nor is the sin of 11:1-9 so drastic as the intermixing of the human and divine in 6:1-4."

14. Umberto Cassuto, *From Noah to Abraham: A Commentary on the First Chapters of Genesis II* (Jerusalem: Magnes, 1964), p. 232.

15. Cassuto, pp. 232-34. Speiser, *Studies*, pp. 53-61 has convincingly used this word play to trace the literary origins of the story. We have omitted the Hebrew letters in this excerpt. See also Samuel Kramer, "The 'Babel of Tongues': A Sumerian Version," *JOAS* 88 (1968):108-11.

16. R. McKenzie, "The Divine Soliloquies in Genesis," *CBQ* 17 (1955):284 points out a parallel between this passage and Genesis 3:22: "The motif is again that of impious human ambitions; men are trying to act like gods, raising themselves by their own powers above their proper character and status as men." We would quibble with this. Man's character and status is to be the image of God. He fulfills this through procreation. In the Tower of Babel, in civilization, man is exerting his powers not to fulfill himself as the image of God, but rather to deny himself.

17. J. P. Fokkelman, *Narrative Art in Genesis* (Amsterdam: van Gorcum, 1975), chap. 1, especially p. 23.

18. We are following the adaptation of Y. T. Radday, "Chiasm in Tora," *Linguistica Biblica* 19 (1972):12-23. An earlier chiastic analysis is Isaac M. Kikawada, "The Shape of Genesis 11:1-9," *Rhetorical Criticism*, ed. J. J. Jackson and Martin Kessler, (1974), pp. 18-32.

19. Our structuring of the text is indebted to: E. W. Bullinger, *Companion Bible*, Part 1 (Oxford: Oxford University Press, 1911); Umberto Cassuto, *From Adam to Noah: A Commentary on the First Chapters of Genesis I* (Jerusalem: Magnes, 1944); and Joseph Blenkinsopp, *From Adam to Abraham* (London: Longman & Todd, 1965).

20. As pointed out in W. M. Clark, "The Animal Series in the Primaeval History," *VT* 18 (1968):433-49, this tripartite division of the animal kingdom can be found in Hosea 4:3; Psalm 8; Zephaniah 1:3.

21. Edmond Leach, in *Genesis as Myth and Other Essays* (London: Jonathan Cape, 1969), has clearly anticipated us here. He sees that the first three days created the static world of the dead, while the last three days created the living world of motion. He also sees (p. 15) that "Cain the Gardener and Abel the Herdsman repeat the antithesis between the first three days of creation and the last three days in the story. Abel's living world is more pleasing to God." For a useful treatment of man as "image of God," see D. J. A. Clines, "The Image of God in Man," *Tyndale Bull* 19 (1968):53-103; Allen S. Gilbert, in "Modern Nomads and Prehistoric Pastoralists: The Limits of Analogy," *JANES* 7 (1975):53-71, presents some important limitations to the analogy between modern nomads and the pastoral nomadism that Genesis seems to admire. An important early attempt to explore biblical nomadism is John Flight, "The Nomadic Idea and Ideal in the Old Testament," *JBL* 42 (1932), 158-226. For the contrary view, see W. D. Davies, *The Gospel and the Sand* (Berkeley: University of California Press, 1974), pp. 75-90.

•

CHAPTER IV

One Noah, One Flood: The Coherence of the Genesis Version

1

Genesis 1–11 may have been produced from divergent traditions. No one can deny that possibility with absolute certainty. But we can ask for the evidence on which the postulation of such divergent traditions is based. Clearly we lack extra-biblical evidence that would justify this postulation. We lack the kind of evidence for Genesis 1–11 that Jeffrey Tigay had in abundance for his developmental analysis of the *Gilgamesh Epic*.[1] Indeed, the extra-biblical evidence we surveyed in chapter 2 seems to support a unitary approach to Genesis 1–11. Therefore, the documentary approach to Genesis 1–11 must stand or fall on internal evidence, evidence from within the text itself.

But what did we find when we looked at this internal evidence in the last chapter? We found an author with such complete mastery over his materials (whatever their source) that it makes no literary sense to speak of him as an editor. The evidence commonly used to show that Genesis 1–11 is a literary patchwork does in our opinion—when closely examined and put in its proper context—support the view that Genesis 1–11 is a literary masterpiece by an author of extraordinary skill and subtlety. So much so, that when we think we find this author napping we had better proceed very carefully. As with Homer or Shakespeare, when you think you have seen something wrong, there may well be something wrong with your own eyes. You are more likely to be wrong than either of them.

Nonetheless, there has been an important omission in our discussion of internal evidence. As yet, we have had nothing to say about the detailed arguments for a documentary interpretation of the Noah story. And if the analyst has here decisive evidence for divergent traditions and the editorial process, he would have ample grounds for persisting in his approach to Genesis 1–11. And so the Noah story is crucial once again. Just as all would have been lost earlier had Wellhausen and others not come up with the documentary interpretation of Noah, so now all will be lost if this interpretation does not stand up under closer scrutiny. This time, however, the documentary hypothesis does drown in the flood.

Indeed, to tell the truth, we are not going to attempt an original analysis of the Noah story. Over the past decade the Wellhausen interpretation of Noah has been systematically dismantled by younger scholars. There have been at least a half dozen important contributions here. Typical of these critiques is the one made (almost by the way) in F. I. Andersen's *The Sentence in Biblical Hebrew*.

> Sentences used in the present chapter cut across passages generally assigned to 'J' and 'P' documents. . . . This means that if the documentary hypothesis is valid, some editor has put together scraps of parallel versions of the same story with scissors and paste, and yet has achieved a result which from the point of view of discourse grammar, looks as if it has been made out of whole cloth.[2]

What Andersen has done from his own grammatical specialty, others have done from theirs. Objections to a unitary reading of Noah have, one after another, been explained, and objections to a documentary reading—apparently unanswerable objections—have been, one after another, raised.

Speiser was accurately representing the situation when, in 1964, he wrote that the documentary interpretation of Noah was established beyond doubt, much as Gilbert Murray was accurate in 1934 when he said that no competent scholar believed Homer the single author of *The Iliad*. The wheel has now come full circle in Homer. And anyone who has examined recent studies of Noah will find it hard not to conclude that it is coming full circle here as well. (It is a measure of the strength of the documentary consensus that these specific studies have not been used to challenge the hypothesis in general.)

In the commentary that follows the text is printed in a single column, but those sections customarily attributed to the Priestly source are italicized for easier identification.

6:1 When men began to multiply on the face of the ground, and daughters were born to them, ²the sons of God saw that the daughters of men were fair; and they took to wife such of them as they chose. ³Then the Lord said, "My spirit shall not abide in man for ever, for he is flesh, but his days shall be a hundred and twenty years." ⁴The Nephilim were on the earth in those days, and also afterward, when the sons of God came in to the daughters of men, and they bore children to them. These were the mighty men that were of old, the men of renown.

⁵The Lord saw that the wickedness of man was great in the earth, and that every imagination of the thoughts of his heart was only evil continually. ⁶And the Lord was sorry that he had made man on the earth, and it grieved him to his heart. ⁷So the Lord said, "I will blot out man whom I have created from the face of the ground, man and beast and creeping things and birds of the air, for I am sorry that I have made them." ⁸But Noah found favor in the eyes of the Lord.

⁹*These are the generations of Noah. Noah was a righteous man, blameless in his generation; Noah walked with God.* ¹⁰*And Noah had three sons, Shem, Ham, and Japheth.*

¹¹*Now the earth was corrupt in God's sight, and the earth was filled with violence.* ¹²*And God saw the earth, and behold, it was corrupt; for all flesh had corrupted their way upon the earth.*

Verses 9–12, far from being an alien intrusion on this narrative actually represent a culmination of verbal motifs developed in the first eight verses.

"When men began to multiply on the face of the. *ground*"—the first clause of the first verse sets up a verbal play on the relationship of "man" (*'ādām*) and "ground" (*'adāmāh*). This play emphasizes man as creature, and as creature he is obeying God's will to be fruitful and multiply. (An order given to him in Genesis 1—which is usually attributed to the Priestly source.)

However, the good that was multiplying (*rbb*) in verse 1 has become evil that was becoming great (*rbb*) by verse 5. "Man" (*'ādām*) is now in this verse presented in connection with a broader term than "ground" (*'adāmāh*). Now evil is multiplying in the "earth" (*'ereṣ*).

In the supposedly alien verse 12 this progression is completed. "Earth" (*'ereṣ*) is repeated, but now "man" is replaced with the more general term "all flesh" (*kl bśr*). And so the man/soil motif has been developed in three steps: man/ground: man/earth: all flesh/earth.

And this is not the only progression. In verse 2 the trouble starts when the "sons of God" saw how fair the daughters of men were. Literally they "saw how good" they were. Much as God in creation saw that it was good—a lovely irony if we do not separate that out as a Priestly account. And obviously the Yahwist is playing with a creation parody here (despite the fact that according to the documentary consensus he could not have known Genesis 1–2), for in verse 5 the parody is continued. Now Yahweh sees how great was the evil. Then Noah finds favor in the eyes of Yahweh. And finally God "saw the earth, and behold, it was corrupt; for all flesh had corrupted their way upon the earth." We quote the whole of this verse not only because the intensive "behold" figuratively plays with sight, but also because the conjunction "for" is a translation for *ky*, the very same word which in the earlier sections had been translated as "how."

Note the way this progression is emphasized by the change in divine names. Sons of *God* see good; Yahweh first sees evil, then sees (in Noah) good; finally God sees evil. Everything is beautifully balanced. There is also a nice balance between the "mighty men" of wickedness produced by sons of God entering into those they shouldn't—between them and the sons of Noah produced by the only man of his generation who *walked* with God as he should have.

If all this were not enough, verses 8 and 9, when read in the Hebrew word order, actually seem to form a chiasmus.

> Noah
>> found favor
>>> in the eyes of the LORD
>>>> *These are the generations of Noah*
>>>> *Noah was a righteous man*
>>>> *perfect he was*
>>>> *in his generations*
>>> *with God*
>> walked
> *Noah*

Far from being two different accounts, Genesis 6:1-12 could scarcely be more tightly unified.[3]

But the detailed analyses of this section should not make us lose sight of how good a beginning to a story it is. A long time ago man lived peacefully and productively on the earth, but this very peaceful productivity, this very goodness, attracted a super-human force that entered and disturbed the moral fiber of human society. God then made a decision to curtail the life expectancy of man, but this seemed to have little effect. Thus he resolved to annihilate mankind with all other creatures—but there was one good man, worthy of being saved.

> 6:13 *And God said to Noah, "I have determined to make an end of all flesh; for the earth is filled with violence through them; behold, I will destroy them with the earth.* [14]*Make yourself an ark of gopher wood; make rooms in the ark, and cover it inside and out with pitch.* [15]*This is how you are to make it: the length of the ark three hundred cubits, its breadth fifty cubits, and its height thirty cubits.* [16]*Make a roof for the ark, and finish it to a cubit above; and set the door of the ark in its side; make it with lower, second, and third decks.* [17]*For behold, I will bring a flood of waters upon the earth, to destroy all flesh in which is the breath of life from under heaven; everything that is on the earth shall die.* [18]*But I will establish my covenant with you; and you shall come into the ark, you, your sons, your wife, and your sons' wives with you.* [19]*And of every living thing of all flesh, you shall bring two of every sort into the ark, to keep them alive with you; they shall be male and female.* [20]*Of the birds according to their kinds, and of the animals according to their kinds, of every creeping thing of the ground according to its kind, two of every sort shall come in to you, to keep them alive.* [21]*Also take with you every sort of food that is eaten, and store it up; and it shall serve as food for you and for them."* [22]*Noah did this; he did all that God commanded him.*
>
> [7:1]*Then the Lord said to Noah, "Go into the ark, you and all your household, for I have seen that you are righteous before me in this generation.* [2]*Take with you seven pairs of all clean animals, the male and his mate; and a pair of the animals that are not clean, the male and his mate;* [3]*and seven pairs of the birds of the air also, male and female, to keep their kind alive upon the face of all the earth.* [4]*For in seven days I will send rain upon the earth forty days and forty nights; and every living thing that I have made I will blot out from the face of the ground."* [5]*And Noah did all that the Lord had commanded him.*

In 6:1-12 we found no evidence in favor of its being composed of two different accounts. Therefore, we need not presume that 6:13–7:5 is itself a duality. If we do not presume such a duality, then a unified reading is fairly obvious.

In 6:13–6:21 God orders Noah to build the ark according to certain specifications, and explains why. (God *will* bring a flood and then you *will* load the ark.) In 6:22 Noah does what he had been ordered to do—namely, he builds the ark according to God's specifications and awaits God's next move. In 7:1-4, Yahweh informs Noah that the second half of the plan is to be implemented. The flood is imminent; Noah is to load the ark as ordered. But now there are further specifications. Noah is now told to bring more animals on board—specifically, seven pairs of all clean animals and seven pairs of birds.

The careful reader will wonder at this addition. Why does Noah need more clean animals? One answer would be that they are the food mentioned earlier. An easier answer becomes apparent later in the story. As soon as Noah's voyage is over, he sacrifices in thanksgiving clean animals and birds. Without the extras, Noah's sacrifice would have rendered these species extinct. So there are no decisive inconsistencies between 6:13-22 and 7:1-5. Neither are there any of the verbal motifs of the kind that weighed so heavily against a documentary reading of 6:1-12. But if the first section of the Noah story favors a unitary reading and the second is neutral, the third section, 7:6-16, is regarded by the analysts as decisively in their favor. In this section Noah, his family, and the animals enter the ark twice.

> 7:6 *Noah was six hundred years old when the flood waters came upon the earth.* [7]And Noah and his sons and his wife and his sons' wives with him went into the ark, to escape the waters of the flood. [8]Of clean animals, and of animals that are not clean, and of birds, and of everything that creeps on the ground, [9]two and two, male and female, went into the ark with Noah, as God had commanded Noah. [10]And after seven days the waters of the flood came upon the earth.
> [11]*In the six hundredth year of Noah's life, in the second month, on the seventeenth day of the month,* on that day all the fountains of the great deep burst forth, and the windows of the heavens were opened. [12]And rain fell upon the earth forty days and forty nights. [13]*On the very same day Noah and his sons, Shem and Ham and*

Japheth, and Noah's wife and the three wives of his sons with them entered the ark, ¹⁴*they and every beast according to its kind, and all the cattle according to their kinds, and every creeping thing that creeps on the earth according to its kind, and every bird according to its kind, every bird of every sort.* ¹⁵*They went into the ark with Noah, two and two of all flesh in which there was the breath of life.* ¹⁶*And they that entered, male and female of all flesh, went in as God had commanded him; and the Lord shut him in.*

The documentary analysts, in order to preserve their hypothesis, have to jump back and forth in this section. Here, not surprisingly, they cannot agree among themselves about a number of verses, and here too the more daring, like von Rad, will momentarily forget about the passivity of the editor, and have him fiddling with the order of his sources. They claim that a justification of this can be found even internally within this passage because of the obvious duplication: Noah, his family, and the animals enter the ark twice. But could this repetition be for emphasis, as when the psalmist writes, "The voice of the Lord breaks the cedars, the Lord breaks the cedars of Lebanon" (Ps. 29:5)?

In Genesis 7:6-10 the author states generally what happened: when Noah was six hundred, he and his family and the animals went on the ark and the flood came. A common way to repeat for emphasis, if one has decided not to repeat verbatim, is to repeat with greater detail. (Ugaritic poetry tends to repeat verbatim; Hebrew poetry tends to repeat with variation.) And so the second time Noah is six hundred, but the precise date is given—the equivalent of February seventeenth. We get the names of his sons and much more zoological information. Moreover, notice the repetition with variation even within this particular boarding. Noah and his family enter in verse 13. The animals enter in verse 14. They all enter again in verse 15. And they all enter again in verse 16—animals on parade. And this time the flood waters do not just come; this time we get the meteorological explanation: "all the fountains of the deep burst forth, and the windows of the heavens were opened." This added detail is perfectly appropriate for the second account, but the analysts have to attribute it to the Priestly source because of its obvious reference to the firmament, which was created in Genesis 1 (long after the Yahwist had gone to the Lord).

Martin Kessler, who is sensitive to Hebrew use of numerology, finds an interesting pattern of verbal repetition operating between the two accounts of the boarding.

> While the divine command has the compound adjective *mikkol* and the preposition *min*, the first execution account uses the preposition *min* three times, suggesting the process of selection, while the second has *kol* six times expressing the completeness of the representation which is finally summed up by the phrase *mikkol-(hab) básar:* the divine command has been executed to perfection![4]

The analyst may well be able to excise references to the firmament from the otherwise Yahwist account. He can do nothing with any number of other words characteristically Priestly. Kessler has pointed out half a dozen words in the Yahwist boarding account that are usually taken as characteristic vocabulary in the Priestly creation account. Moreover, "clean and unclean," which earlier was taken as a peculiarly Yahwist distinction, is found in both the Yahwist and the Priestly accounts of the boarding. If the analyst then tries gamely to excise the clean animals from the Priestly account (a trade of the clean animals for the firmament?), to do so he has to introduce into the Yahwist version the very kind of repetition he earlier took as a sign of diverse sources. (Perhaps we are on the way to discovering a deutero–Yahwist.) All of this just to avoid admitting that perhaps the two accounts of the boarding are there for the sake of emphasis, much as the multiple boardings of the animals between verses 14–6. Clearly, 7:6–15 does not support a documentary reading very easily—and indeed seems to cause considerable trouble for the documentary analysis of the previous section, an analysis (as we noted) which internally seemed at least as plausible as a unitary one.

And then, of course, there is the concluding part of verse 16. "And they that entered, male and female of all flesh, went in as God had commanded him; and the Lord shut him in." We noted earlier how awkward this particular verse is for the documentary analyst who, Solomon-like, must split it in half. But, of course, wise Solomon did not split the baby, and we needn't split the verse.

Entering the ark is the culminating episode of this whole part of the story. If an author had been skillfully moving back and forth between two different divine names throughout the earlier sections of the story (as it seems to us he has), then one way for him to verbally signify a climax would be to bring these two names together. And this is just what he does.

Such a doubling of divine names within a single passage resembles very closely the use of divine names in Akkadian epic narratives such as in the two consecutive lines from Atrahasis where the creatress of man is called by two of her many names:

> Nine days let the brick be in place
> May *Nintu*, the mother-womb, be honored.
> *Mami* their . . . proclaim without ceasing,
> Without ceasing praise the birth-goddess,
> Praise Kesh![5]

And, in the Akkadian Creation Epic we find the creator of man, Enki, referred to by two different names:

> After *Ea*, the wise, had created mankind,
> Had imposed upon it the service of the gods.
> That work was beyond the comprehension
> As artfully planned by Marduk, did *Nudimmud* create it.[6]

A similar phenomenon is also observed in certain Ugaritic narratives; for example:

> Qdš-and-Amrr embraces
> He sets Asherah on the back of the ass
> On the beautiful back of the donkey.
> *Qdš* begins to light the way
> Even *Amrr*, like a star.[7]

Here the name(s) of a deity, Qdš-and-Amrr, is separated and distributed to the two parallel lines. A further example from the Ugaritic is:

> Unto thee (is) *Ktr*, thy companion
> Yea *Hss*, thine acquaintance!
> In the sea is Arš and Tannîn.
> *Ktr-and-Hss* proceeds
> *Ktr-and-Hss* leaves.[8]

Here *Ktr* and *Hss* are introduced separately and then joined to make the full name of one deity.

But, of course, this does not establish that a Hebrew author, especially one who used Elohim and Yahweh together in the Adam and Eve story rather consistently, would pull them together for the sake of climax here. Perhaps we should then point out that the final climax of the Noah story occurs when Noah himself speaks for the very first time. He utters a curse and then utters a blessing. The blessing begins, "Blessed be Yahweh, Elohim of Shem."

But this fuss over the divine names should not distract us from an important methodological issue that our treatment of this passage would raise in the mind of any follower of Noth or von Rad. We have been confronted with a repeated occurrence of the same event in different versions. We have pointed out that such a repetition could be the result of an author seeking emphasis, not an editor fumbling with divergent traditions. It would be the narrative equivalent of what the ancient Romans would call an *accumulatio,* a common literary device. But Noth, in particular, would think that in so interpreting a narrative repetition we were making a methodological mistake of a most rudimentary kind. If Noth is right, then our reading of this text could be rejected, almost *a prioi*. Since many biblical critics (albeit fewer and fewer Classicists) would agree with Noth on this, we must pause in our analysis of the Noah story to examine this methodological presupposition.

2

It seems to be that fundamentally only one of the usual criteria for the disunity of the old Pentateuchal tradition is really useful, though this one is quite adequate and allows a thoroughgoing literary analysis. I refer to the unquestionable fact, attested time and again throughout the tradition, of *repeated occurrence* of the same narrative materials or narrative elements in *different versions.* The phenomenon can hardly be explained in any other way.[9]

So Martin Noth states his position with his characteristic frankness and clarity.

Despite all of Noth's immense learning and his many important contributions to biblical studies, his attempt here to make his methodological presupposition explicit only makes it more questionable. We have no doubt that sometimes repetition in different versions is a sign of divergent traditions. Nor do we deny that a literary critic should consider this possibility when confronted with repetition, especially in works which originated in oral transmission. But to say that the phenomenon can scarcely be explained in any other way is to say something obviously false. Nonetheless, since this false principle is widely regarded as self-evidently true, we must examine it in more detail than it may merit. Only then will we feel free to return to the Noah story.

Repetition, after all, is one of the most fundamental tools of the literary artist, either oral or written. And this is why the Greek and Roman rhetorical traditions developed such an elaborate terminology to classify the different kinds of repetition: *Repetitio mater studiorum*. Robert Alter states one possible function of repetition for an ancient Hebrew:

> If you were a Judean herdsman standing in the outer circle of listeners while the story of the Ten Plagues was being read, you might miss a few phrases when God instructs Moses about turning the Nile into blood (Exodus 7:17-18), but you could easily pick up what you had lost when the instructions were almost immediately repeated verbatim as narrated action (Exod. 7:20-21). If you were close enough to the reader to catch every word, you could still enjoy the satisfaction of hearing each individual term of God's grim prediction, first stated in the prophetic future, then restated as accomplished fact, with an occasional elegant variation.[10]

Calum Carmichael makes a similar point with respect to the law codes of Deuteronomy:

> The frequent repetition of rules for sacrifice and worship does not suggest a heterogenous code of rules, composed at different times and places, but rather reflects a setting of instruction. Matters are repeated, especially in this opening part of instruction, in order to fix the teaching in the mind of the hearer.[11]

What both Carmichael and Alter suggest is that we judge a passage not in terms of some abstract notion of our own but rather in terms of its intended effect on an audience. Once we approach the passage not philosophically but rhetorically, what seemed to us as redundant or conceptually unnecessary becomes rather a measure of the author's skill.

Now let us take what Noth regards as his own best examples. They are from the Abraham story. In Genesis 15-18 God makes a formal covenant with Abraham no less than three times: different traditions about the same event, says Noth, an event so important the editor did not feel able to omit any insignificant version. In Genesis 12 and 20, Sarah/Sarai is twice passed off as Abraham/Abram's sister; in Genesis 14 and then again in 19 Lot is saved from grief. These are other cases where divergent traditions have been spliced together.

Possibly Noth's interpretations of these episodes are correct, but they are far from being as obviously correct as he seems to think. Let us take the triple covenant to start with.

Much as an editor might want to include all variants of the story, so an author might well want to repeat it to give it suitable emphasis. How many times should he repeat it? Well, there were three aspects of the covenant. It was a covenant *with* Abraham, *for* both land and innumerable seed. So we would have three versions, one emphasizing Abraham, another the land, and another the seed. What order should they be in? Since the story itself is of Abraham's relationship with God, that version of the covenant should be in the middle. Since Abraham has already seen the land that will be his people's but has yet to see the first of his seed, perhaps the land-emphasizing covenant should be first and the seed-emphasizing last. (And in a more general sense land is required before seed can be sown.) But the order of these two episodes is less important since they are in a way parallel.

We are not saying that this is the correct interpretation of the triple covenant, but only that it is at least as plausible on the surface as the hypothesis of differing traditions. Things are not as easy for the analyst as Noth would have us believe.

What about the other episodes? These are a little more complicated to explain, but not much. We have already seen how Genesis 6:8-9 was ordered in a chiasmus. Later in the Noah story there is a three-verse chiasmus:

A   And all flesh died that moved upon the earth
  B   birds, cattle, beasts, all swarming creatures that swarm upon
     the earth
    C   and every man
      D   everything on the dry land in whose nostrils was the
        breath of life
        E   died;
          F   He
        E   blotted out
      D   every
    C   Man
  B   and animals and creeping things and birds of the air;
A   they were blotted out from the earth.[12]

Obviously an author who takes pleasure in such local chiasmuses might well try to extend them to larger and larger passages. We have already seen that the Tower of Babel story is itself a chiasmus.

How large can such chiasmuses get? In theory there seems no limit. In one of the impressive recent contributions to our understanding of *The Iliad*'s unity, Whitman has shown how the whole work constitutes a single gigantic chiasmus.[13] Less ambitiously, we shall turn to the sequence of the repeated episodes in the Abraham story.

Note now how the repeated stories are arranged in the larger tale of Abraham.

    Sarai and the Pharaoh (chapter 12)
      The saving of Lot (chapter 14)
        Covenant for land (chapter 15)
          Covenant with Abraham (chapter 17)
        Covenant for seed (chapter 18)
      The rescue of Lot (chapter 19)
    Sarah and Abimelech (chapter 20)

The chiastic structuring of the events seems fairly obvious and is nicely reinforced by the triple covenant. And if we compare, for instance, the two episodes of Sarah, we find the differences between them functional for the larger story of Abraham.

What is striking about these stories of Sarah when they are placed side-by-side is that the second story is consistently amplified to soften the first. In the first, Sarai goes into the Pharaoh's house and the implication is that she has sexual relations with him; in the second we are specifically told that Abimelech did not touch her. In the first the Pharaoh is punished "with great plagues" for his taking Sarai; in the second Abimelech is preserved from any punishment beyond the temporary barrenness of his women. In the first the Pharaoh apparently infers what has happened himself; in the second Abimelech is informed specifically by Yahweh. In the first Abram, when accused, says nothing; in the second Abraham is allowed to explain away his lie by casuistry. Abram is summarily sent away; Abraham is allowed to stay in friendship after he has interceded for Abimelech.[14]

We could have two divergent traditions, but we could also have a skillful author trying to teach his people the difference it makes to have a covenant with God. He dramatizes this difference by having the same situation occur twice—once before the covenant, once after. What in the documentary interpretation is taken as evidence of literary primitivism is in the second an example of literary skill. Only by a detailed examination of the Abraham story as a whole will we be able to decide between these two possible interpretations. We obviously do not have space to defend a chiastic interpretation of the Abraham story. The following diagram will at least indicate how it might be done.

A   Abram's Call; Promise of Seed (11:31–12:3)
    B   Sojourn in Canaan (12:4-9)
       C   Sojourn in Egypt; Denial of Sarai (12:10-20)
          D   Separation of Lot; Manifestation of Land (13:1-18)
             E   War on Sodom; Rescue of Lot by Abram (14:1-24)
                F   Covenant Made: Land (15:1-21)
                   G   Sarai's Effort (16:1-16)
                     H   Covenant Made: Abraham (17:1-14)
                   G   Sarah's Blessing (17:15-27)
                F   Covenant Made: Seed (18:1-15)
             E   Destruction of Sodom; Rescue of Lot by Angels (18:16–19:38)
       C   Sojourn in Gerar; Denial of Sarah (20:1-18)
          D   Manifestation of Seed; Separation of Ishmael (21:1-21)
    B   Sojourn in Gerar (21:22-34)
A   Abraham's Test: Blessing of Seed (22:1-19)[15]

To assert initially that such repetitions can hardly be explained other than by the documentary hypothesis is, to put it kindly, hyperbole.

3

7:17 The flood continued forty days upon the earth; and the waters increased, and bore up the ark, and it rose high above the earth. ¹⁸*The waters prevailed and increased greatly upon the earth; and the ark floated on the face of the waters. ¹⁹And the waters prevailed so mightily upon the earth that all the high mountains under the whole heaven were covered; ²⁰the waters prevailed above the mountains, covering them fifteen cubits deep. ²¹And all flesh died that moved upon the earth, birds, cattle, beasts, all swarming creatures that swarm upon the earth, and every man;* ²²everything on the dry land in whose nostrils was the breath of life died. ²³He blotted out every living thing that was upon the face of the ground, man and animals and creeping things and birds of the air; they were blotted out from the earth. Only Noah was left, and those that were with him in the ark. ²⁴*And the waters prevailed upon the earth a hundred and fifty days.*

⁸:¹*But God remembered Noah and all the beasts and all the cattle that were with him in the ark. And God made a wind blow over the earth, and the waters subsided;* ²*the fountains of the deep and the windows of the heavens were closed,* the rain from the heavens was restrained, ³and the waters receded from the earth continually. *At the end of a hundred and fifty days the waters had abated;* ⁴*and in the seventh month, on the seventeenth day of the month, the ark came to rest upon the mountains of Ararat.* ⁵*And the waters continued to abate until the tenth month; in the tenth month, on the first day of the month, the tops of the mountains were seen.*

Cassuto's translation of vs. 17–19 makes more apparent the beautiful verbal formalism that stretches across the alleged seam between verses 17 and 18.[16]

17. And the flood continued / forty days / upon the earth, and the waters increased, / and bore up the ark, / and it was lifted up above the earth.

18. The waters prevailed / and increased greatly / upon the earth; and the ark floated / on the face of the waters.

19. And the waters / prevailed so mightily / upon the earth
    that all the high mountains / under the whole heaven / were covered.

The technical name for this figure of speech—the repetition of the same word or phrase at the end of successive phrases—is epistrophe. We can find it in Genesis 13:6: "And the land was not able to bear them, that they might dwell together: for their substance was great, so that they could not dwell together." Or in the Hebrew of Deuteronomy 2:10: "In a desert land He found him / And in the waste howling wilderness, about, he led him. As the apple of His eye He kept him."

It has long been a commonplace of biblical criticism to regard this section as the center of the Noah story, whether the story is analyzed as a unified or dualistic work. We watch the waters come and prevail, and then we watch them recede. This general sense is reinforced by the return of the root *rbb* ("to multiply, be great"). We saw how important this root was at the beginning of the story—and it is now thematically important once again.

At the beginning of the story man began to multiply (*rbb*) on the face of the earth, but then made great (*rbb*) evil in the sight of God. Now as a punishment for that, evil man is blotted out by the multiplying (*rbb*) forces of water. "The waters increased (*rbb*), and bore up the ark, and it rose high above the earth. The waters prevailed and increased greatly (*rbb*) upon the earth." Twice at the beginning, twice in the middle—if the Noah story is the work of a single, consummate literary artist, we expect the root *rbb* to appear twice again, near the end of the story. And this expectation is fulfilled. The final destination of *rbb* is the divine blessing at the end. And at this conclusion, it is there not just twice, but four times (twice two). These blessings are, after all, the end, the sum, the culmination of all that has gone before—or so the author seems to be telling us.

An author as skillful as this would certainly be alive to the chiastic possibilities of the flood story, the coming and receding of the waters being imitated by a balanced organization of the story itself. The exact center—the moment at which the waters are at their maximum, the moment before the waters begin to recede—is expressed in the text in the verse: "But God remembered Noah and all the beasts that were with him in the ark." This is the central moment in the flood, but is it the literary center of a chiasmus? We can only start from this hypothetical center and work out looking for parallels. And these parallels are not difficult to find. [17]

The waters abate after one hundred fifty days (8:2-3); for one hundred fifty days the waters prevail (7:21-4). The ark lands and the tops of mountains are seen (8:4-5); the ark is adrift and the tops of mountains are covered (7:18-20). Clearly there is a chiasmus here. The only question is how far it extends.

8:6 At the end of forty days Noah opened the window of the ark which he had made, [7]*and sent forth a raven; and it went to and fro until the waters were dried up from the earth.* [8]Then he sent forth a dove from him, to see if the waters had subsided from the face of the ground; [9]but the dove found no place to set her foot, and she returned to him to the ark, for the waters were still on the face of the whole earth. So he put forth his hand and took her and brought her into the ark with him. [10]He waited another seven days, and again he sent forth the dove out of the ark; [11]and the dove came back to him in the evening, and lo, in her mouth a freshly plucked olive leaf; so Noah knew that the waters had subsided from the earth. [12]Then he waited another seven days, and sent forth the dove; and she did not return to him any more.
[13]*In the six hundred and first year, in the first month, the first day of the month,* the waters were dried from off the earth; and *Noah removed the covering of the ark, and looked, and behold, the face of the ground was dry.* [14]*In the second month, on the twenty-seventh day of the month, the earth was dry.* [15]*Then God said to Noah,* [16]*"Go forth from the ark, you and your wife, and your sons and your sons' wives with you.* [17]*Bring forth with you every living thing that is with you of all flesh—birds and animals and every creeping thing that creeps on the earth—that they may breed abundantly on the earth, and be fruitful and multiply upon the earth."* [18]*So Noah went forth, and his sons and his wife and his sons' wives with him.* [19]*And every beast, every creeping thing, and every bird, everything that moves upon the earth, went forth by families out of the ark.*
[20]Then Noah built an altar to the Lord, and took of every clean animal and of every clean bird, and offered burnt offerings on the altar. [21]And when the Lord smelled the pleasing odor, the Lord said in his heart, "I will never again curse the ground because of man, for the imagination of man's heart is evil from his youth; neither will

I ever again destroy every living creature as I have done. ²²While the earth remains, seedtime and harvest, cold and heat, summer and winter, day and night, shall not cease."

The chiasmus continues. In 8:6 Noah opens a window of the ark after forty days of waiting while in 7:16-7 before forty days of flood Yahweh shuts the ark. In 8:7-9 a dove and raven leave the ark; in 7:11-15 the animals enter the ark, including "every bird according to its kind, every bird of every sort." We note that 8:10-12 describes two seven-day waiting periods, as does 7:4-10. More important, Noah enters the ark in 7:6-10 because God ordered him and God resolved to "blot out from the face of all the earth" every living thing that God had made. In 8:13-17, Noah is ordered to leave the ark; he obeys (18-19); and God vows never again to destroy everything He has made (20-22).[18]

> 9:1 *And God blessed Noah and his sons, and said to them, "Be fruitful and multiply, and fill the earth. ²The fear of you and the dread of you shall be upon every beast of the earth, and upon every bird of the air, upon everything that creeps on the ground and all the fish of the sea; into your hand they are delivered. ³Every moving thing that lives shall be food for you; and as I gave you the green plants, I give you everything. ⁴Only you shall not eat flesh with its life, that is, its blood. ⁵For your lifeblood I will surely require a reckoning; of every beast I will require it and of man; of every man's brother I will require the life of man. ⁶Whoever sheds the blood of man, by man shall his blood be shed; for God made man in his own image. ⁷And you, be fruitful and multiply, bring forth abundantly on the earth and multiply in it."*
>
> *⁸Then God said to Noah and to his sons with him, ⁹"Behold, I establish my covenant with you and your descendants after you, ¹⁰and with every living creature that is with you, the birds, the cattle, and every beast of the earth with you, as many as came out of the ark. ¹¹I establish my covenant with you, that never again shall flesh be cut off by the waters of flood, and never again shall there be a flood to destroy the earth." ¹²And God said, "This is the sign of the covenant which I make between me and you and every living creature that is with you, for all future generations: ¹³I set my bow in the cloud, and it shall be a sign of the covenant between me and the earth. ¹⁴When I bring clouds over the earth and the bow is seen in the clouds, ¹⁵I will remember my covenant which is between me and you and every living creature of all flesh; and the waters shall never again become a flood to destroy all flesh. ¹⁶When the bow is in the clouds, I will look upon it and remember the everlasting*

covenant between God and every living creature of all flesh that is upon the earth." [17]*God said to Noah, "This is the sign of the covenant which I have established between me and all flesh that is upon the earth."*

[18]The sons of Noah who went forth from the ark were Shem, Ham, and Japheth. Ham was the father of Canaan. [19]These three were the sons of Noah; and from these the whole earth was peopled.

[20]Noah was the first tiller of the soil. He planted a vineyard; [21]and he drank of the wine, and became drunk, and lay uncovered in his tent. [22]And Ham, the father of Canaan, saw the nakedness of his father, and told his two brothers outside. [23]Then Shem and Japheth took a garment, laid it upon both their shoulders, and walked backward and covered the nakedness of their father; their faces were turned away, and they did not see their father's nakedness. [24]When Noah awoke from his wine and knew what his youngest son had done to him, [25]he said,
"Cursed be Canaan;
    a slave of slaves shall he be to his brothers."
[26]He also said,
"Blessed by the Lord my god be Shem;
    and let Canaan be his slave.
[27]God enlarge Japheth,
    and let him dwell in the tents of Shem;
    and let Canaan be his slave."
[28]*After the flood Noah lived three hundred and fifty years.* [29]*All the days of Noah were nine hundred and fifty years; and he died.*

The parallels between 9:1-19 and 6:10-21 are fairly obvious. There is the food on the ark (6:21) and the food outside (9:2-4); the covenant with Noah (6:18-20) and the covenant with all flesh (9:8-10); the prophecy of the flood (6:17) and the promise of no future flood (9:11-5); the ark of the flood (6:14-6) and the rainbow of the floodless future (9:16-7); Noah and his sons Shem, Ham, and Japheth (6:1-10); and Noah and his sons Shem, Ham, and Japheth (9:18-9). Some of these parallels do cause trouble for the documentary hypothesis; for instance, the last one concerning Noah's sons has to go across documents. But that should cause little surprise, since almost every passage in the Noah story when closely examined causes trouble for the documentary hypothesis.

What is striking about these parallels is that they suggest we can extend the chiasmus to the strange story of Noah, his drunkenness, and his sons. We have earlier shown how tightly the equally strange story about the sons of God is tied to the beginning of the Noah story. It seems a prologue to the flood story. Our chiastic analysis suggests a parallel to the story of Noah's vineyard—the epilogue to the flood story.

Let us start with the working assumption that the epilogue, no less than the prologue, has to do with procreation. This is not so strange an assumption. After all, Noah has just been told to be fruitful and multiply. And we have just been told that Noah and his sons were going to obey the command, for "from these the whole earth was peopled."

Why was Noah's first recorded act after the renewed covenant with God the planting of a vineyard? This, we might suggest, was the old sedentary sin. But we can understand why Noah was tempted. Noah was righteous but very old. The wine was his way to rekindle diminished sexual desire. We do not need to quote similes from the Song of Songs ("your kisses like the best wine") to establish that in the ancient Near East—and in other times and places as well—alcohol increases sexual desire and also lessens inhibitions. Nonetheless, anyone who has understood why God rejected Cain's fruits (and his way of life) will anticipate that no good will come from this cultivation of the land—indeed, that it will result in disrespect for procreation in some sense. We do not have to wait long for our expectation to be fulfilled, for soon Ham sees Noah's nakedness in his tent. What does this mean?

In fact, "his tent" is a questionable translation; the noun has an ending that suggests "her tent." Hence rabbinic scholars have interpreted the passage as referring to the tent of Noah's wife. Leviticus 18:8 is worth quoting here: "You shall not uncover the nakedness of your father's wife; it is your father's nakedness."

Ham perhaps sees his father and mother in an act of intercourse, or at least attempted intercourse. We must note here that Noah will have no more children. He is no longer potent. But why should Ham celebrate what he has seen? And why should Noah, after sleeping off his inebriation, curse not Ham but Ham's son? The parallel episode with the sons of God may be of some help here.

In this episode there was illicit sexual activity, activity which violated the natural order. The flood was God's curse on the issue from this union, the mighty and renowned men of old. In contrast with the curse, God blessed his good "son" Noah, much as Noah himself would bless his good sons. If these parallels are correct (and the general chiastic structure of the Flood story leads us to think that they probably are), then Canaan would be cursed as the product of illicit sexual intercourse by Ham. Certainly the line of Ham produced men of renown—among them Nimrod, "the first on earth to be a mighty man," whose kingdom is associated with "Babel" and "Accad" (Babylon and Akkadia?).

If Canaan is the product of illicit intercourse by Ham, when and with whom did it occur? One answer suggests itself. Ham commits incest with his mother after his father is rendered incapacitated by drink (and after Noah arouses the mother but proves incapable of satisfying her). Ham supplants his father, much as the sons of God before supplanted other potential human fathers.

This interpretation of an enigmatic story seems plausible.[19] We propose it not because we think we have presented decisive arguments in its favor, but only because it shows how the recognition of chiastic structure can shed light on the most obscure of stories. The episode of Noah's drunkenness is not intended to make sense considered by itself, but only as a part of a larger whole—and especially in juxtaposition to its parallel episode of the sons of God.

Nonetheless, the parallels between the episodes of Noah's drunkenness and the sons of God are less important for our purposes than recognizing the unity of the Noah story to which they provide the frame. And no one has set out this structural unity better than Wenham. (See next page.)

Whether we look at the chiastic structure as a whole, or specific repetitions like the boardings of the ark or alleged seams like 6:8-9, the result is always the same. There is no good reason for a documentary interpretation, many reasons for the story as a coherent whole. We have incorporated the observations of the documentary analysts into our own reading, and we have left their interpretation of the evidence far behind. All that is left for us to do is to begin to explore the implications of a unified Genesis 1–11 for our understanding of the rest of the Bible.

"A Noah (vi. 10a)
B   Shem, Ham, and Japheth (10b)
C   Ark to be built (14-16)
D   Flood announced (17)
E   Covenant with Noah (18-20)
F   Food in the ark (21)
G   Command to enter ark (vii. 1-3)
H   7 days waiting for flood (4-5)
I   7 days waiting for flood (7-10)
J   Entry to ark (11-15)
K   Yahweh shuts Noah in (16)
L   40 days flood (17a)
M   Waters increase (17b-18)
N   Mountains covered (19-20)
O   150 days waters prevail (21-24)
P   GOD REMEMBERS NOAH (viii. 1)
O'   150 days waters abate (3)
N'   Mountain tops visible (4-5)
M'   Waters abate (5)
L'   40 days (end of) (6a)
K'   Noah opens window of ark (6b)
J'   Raven and dove leave ark (7-9)
I'   7 days waiting for waters to subside (10-11)
H'   7 days waiting for waters to subside (12-13)
G'   Command to leave ark (15-17 [22])
F'   Food outside ark (ix. 1-4)
E'   Covenant with all flesh (8-10)
D'   No flood in future (11-17)
C'   Ark (18a)
B'   Shem, Ham, and Japheth (18b)
A' Noah (19)"[20]

Notes / Chapter IV

1. Jeffrey H. Tigay, *The Evolution of the Gilgamesh Epic* (Philadelphia: University of Pennsylvania Press, 1982). Perhaps we should point out parenthetically that even if we could establish with certainty that Genesis 1–11 was the product of a single author, the developmental approach might still be useful. We could try to infer the stages of the author's composition of the text, attributing this or that section of the text to early or later drafts. Thus the descendants of Wilamowitz occupy themselves with so indisputable a single-author text as Virgil's *Aeneid*. See, for instance, Gordon Williams, *Technique and Ideas in the Aeneid* (New Haven: Yale University Press, 1983), appendix.

2. Francis I. Andersen, *The Sentence in Biblical Hebrew* (The Hague: Mouton, 1974). Beyond Andersen we have found the following studies of the Flood story especially helpful: B. W. Anderson, "From Analysis of Synthesis:

The Interpretation of Genesis 1–11," *JBL* 97 (1978):23-29; W. M. Clark, "The Animal Series in the Primaeval History," *VT* 18 (1968):433-49; Sean E. McEvenue, *The Narrative Style of the Priestly Writer* (Rome: Pontifical Biblical Institute, 1971); and especially Gordon J. Wenham, "The Coherence of the Flood Narrative," *VT* 28 (1978):336-48. Quite frankly, these works so strongly support our argument we have shied away from offering any original interpretation, although we suspect that the Noah story has a more complex unity than even suggested by these fine studies. See Kikawada, *Antediluvian Historiography*, pp. 41-124.

3. Emil Kraeling, "The Significance and Origin of Genesis 6:1-4," *JANES* 6 (1947):193-203, argues on quite different grounds that Genesis 6:1-4 presumes the existence of the Flood story. He argues against the Wellhausen interpretation, which treats it as a separate unit.

4. Jackson and Kessler, *Rhetorical Criticism*, pp. 1-17.

5. W. G. Lambert and A. R. Millard, *Atra-Hasis: The Babylonian Story of the Flood with The Sumerian Flood Story* by Miguel Civil (Oxford: Oxford University Press, 1969), I:294-98.

6. James Pritchard, ed., *Ancient Near Eastern Texts* (Princeton: Princeton University Press, 1950), pp. 60-72.

7. Cyrus Gordon, *Ugaritic Textbook* (Rome: Pontifical Biblical Institute, 1965), 51:IV, pp. 13-17.

8. Gordon, 62:49.

9. Martin Noth, *Pentateuchal Traditions*, p. 21.

10. Robert Alter, *The Art of Biblical Narrative* (New York: Basic Books, 1981), pp. 90-91.

11. Calum Carmichael, *The Laws of Deuteronomy* (Ithaca: Cornell University Press, 1974), p. 69.

12. This is observed in what is undoubtedly the best study of biblical chiasmus: Nils Wilhelm Lund, *Chiasmus in the New Testament* (Chapel Hill: University of North Carolina Press, 1942), p. 60.

13. Cedric Whitman, *Homer and the Heroic Tradition* (Cambridge, Mass.: Harvard University Press, 1958). See also for another long chiasmus, this one from a Mesopotamian source, Anne Kilmer, "A Note on an Overlooked Wordplay." *Zikir Sumim* (Leiden, the Netherlands: E. J. Brill, 1982).

14. An interesting attempt to explain Abraham's behavior is E. A. Speiser, *Studies*, pp. 62-82.

15. This is based on E. W. Bullinger, *Companion Bible*, Part I (Oxford: Oxford University Press, 1911), p. 18. Of course, we would also have to explain Isaac's denial of *his* wife.

16. Umberto Cassuto, *From Noah to Abraham: A Commentary on the First Chapters of Genesis II* (Jerusalem: Magnes, 1964), p. 92.

17. A chiastic structure for the Flood story was suggested by Lund, *Chiasmus*. Of the more recent attempts we find most persuasive Anderson, "From Analysis," and especially Wenham, "Coherence."

18. The anthropomorphism of God "smelling the pleasing odor" in the Wellhausen interpretation has been taken as a sure sign of the theological primitivism of the Yahwist, as opposed to the Priestly writer who is more like us. But we must raise the question whether or not obvious theological anthropomorphism is itself a sure sign of backwardness. McKenzie in his fine study of the Divine soliloquies in Genesis does well to insist, "It should be stressed, and students should be reminded, that any affirmation concerning God that can be made in human language is to a greater or lesser degree

anthropomorphic and metaphorical. . . . In reality, the statement that 'God is spirit' (John 4:24) is not less anthropomorphic than 'the just shall behold his face' (Psalm 11:7). The difference is merely that the one has used a spiritual part of man, the other a physical, as a *primum analogatum* for a truth about God." R. McKenzie, "The Divine Soliloquies in Genesis, *CBQ* 17 (1955):157-58. The difference between the two analogies is that the former is more refined—and for that reason it is, at least in one respect, more dangerous because we can forget more easily its analogical nature. We can therefore easily understand why a sophisticated author might prefer to write about God in the most obvious anthropomorphisms.

19. Our interpretation is influenced by F. W. Bassett, "Noah's Nakedness and the Curse of Canaan: A Case of Incest?" *VT* 21 (1971):232-37, and H. H. Cohen, *The Drunkenness of Noah* (Mobile: University of Alabama Press, 1974), although the latter reaches far different conclusions.

20. Wenham, "Coherence." He also persuasively refutes the claim that two incompatible chronologies govern the story.

CHAPTER V

•

After Abraham Was: Genesis 1–11 as a Paradigm of Biblical Unity

1

To understand properly the structure and content of the Pentateuch as a whole and in its details, one must attempt to penetrate into the early stages of the history of its traditions. In this respect, the situation in the Pentateuch is completely different from that of the great literary histories found in the Old Testament. As literary works, these *originated* on the basis of literary activity. Granted, these works frequently absorbed traditions with a long prehistory of their own, whose origins reached back into the stages of oral transmission—as is the case at least with the Deuteronomistic History. Nevertheless, in each case they owe their existence *as a whole*, their arrangement and structure, to the work of a particular writer, the "author," who had at hand the earlier traditions and complexes of traditions as literary sources and who, by using these sources, composed and arranged the work as a whole for the first and last time. In these cases the understanding of the total work must begin with an analysis of the work of each particular "author." The Pentateuch, on the other hand, does not have an "author" in this sense at all.[1]

So Martin Noth grandly summarizes one implication of the documentary hypothesis. There should be a discontinuity between a literary history—such as those of Saul, David, Solomon, and their successors—and Pentateuchal histories such as that contained in Genesis. Our approach suggests exactly the opposite; it emphasizes the continuity between the Pentateuchal and the "literary" histories. We think that they had authors in much the same sense. How might we explore this possibility?

107

How might we test the contrary predictions of our hypothesis and Noth's?

We have found a distinctive structure in Genesis 1–11 shared with the older epic of Atrahasis. Finding this structure replicated in one of the great histories of the Hebrew monarchy would seem almost too much to hope for—and yet we found just this described in a remarkable article by Walter Brueggemann.[2] The following is an adaptation of his table of parallels between the Genesis primeval history and reign of David and Solomon as recorded in the books of Samuel and Kings. The plots are essentially the same.

I. Adam and Eve:
    Adam takes forbidden fruit.
	David and Bathsheba:
	    David covets the wife of another man.

Adam is aware of his nakedness and is afraid.	David is made aware of his sin and confesses.
Adam is under death sentence, but is not executed.	The death sentence is pronounced upon David but he is not executed.
Adam and his seed is cursed.	The curse of sword is pronounced.
Adam is expelled from the garden.	Loss of the dynasty is suggested.
A son is born to the cursed couple.	A son is born to the cursed couple.

II. Cain and Abel:
    Cain kills Abel in the field.
	Amnon and Absalom:
	    A man kills his brother in the field.

Cain is very angry at his brother.	Absalom hates his brother.
Cain violates the Torah: murder.	Absalom violates the Torah: murder.
Cain fears for his life.	A woman fears for the life of Absalom.

Cain is granted life by God.

Absalom is granted life by David.

Cain must be a wanderer away from the presence of God.

Absalom must dwell apart from David.

Cain is father of arts and crafts.

Absalom is restored to the presence of the King.

III. Noah and the Flood:
Noah's generation is evil.

The Rebellion of Absalom:
Absalom brings evil on the dynasty.

Noah finds favor with God.

David hopes to find favor with God.

God intervenes for Noah.

God intervenes for David.

God resolves to blot out the corrupt.

Absalom is blotted out without an heir.

Ham sees the nakedness of Noah.

Absalom seizes the concubines of David.

God promises a new beginning.

David makes a new beginning.

Noah gives blessings and curses.

David deals with enemies and friends.

IV. The Tower of Babel:
The people want a name.

Solomon:
The name wanted by the dynasty is achieved by Solomon.

The people propose to build a city.

Solomon is the great builder of Jerusalem.

The people are able to do all they devise.

Solomon prospers in all he does.

The guilty are scattered.

Later the dynasty and realm are scattered.

Unfortunately Brueggemann, in our opinion at least, draws exactly the wrong conclusion from his remarkable analysis:

> This is not to deny the background in Canaanite and Mesopotamian myth for the various [Genesis] stories. . . . My point, however, is that this non-Israelite background is not a significant factor in the way the Israelite theologian handles the materials he utilized.

Brueggemann believes that the sequence of events and their themes in the Davidic monarchy were primary and the sequence in the Genesis primeval history secondary. He suggests that the author of Genesis 1–11 was a court theologian celebrating the monarchy. We have shown that this very sequence itself is derived from a common Near Eastern tradition. Clearly, then, the primeval history was being used to give shape to and to make sense of the events of recorded history.

Perhaps we should state that we do not find the priority of myth over history surprising. The most important recent study of modern historiography, Hayden White's *Metahistory: The Historical Imagination in Nineteenth-Century Europe,* argues that historians and philosophers of history will inevitably use myths to prefigure and thereby render intelligible an historical field.[3] White would have us distinguish between the unsophisticated historian who does this unconsciously, and the sophisticated who does it consciously. From White's view, then, whoever wrote the history from David to Solomon might well have been far more sophisticated methodologically than many famous nineteenth-century German historians who prided themselves on their critical capacity.

The parallel between the Tower of Babel and the building of Solomon's Temple does suggest dramatically that the author's view of the monarchy was far from flattering. The Saul-David-Solomon period, of course, represents the great effort of the Hebrews themselves to be the center of a great civilization. The hostility of the prophet Samuel to the original foundation of this monarchy was obvious enough, as was the Lord's. And the eventual naming of the histories after Samuel is appropriate, if we see that his condemnation was meant to extend to Solomon long after the prophet's death. "But the thing displeased Samuel when they said, 'Give us a king to govern us.' And Samuel prayed to the Lord. And the Lord said to Samuel, 'Hearken to the voice of the people in all that they say to you; for they have not rejected

you, but they have rejected me from being king over them"
(8:6-7). The Hebrews, now having become sedentary in the
Promised Land, could not resist the most beautiful fruit at the
center of the garden. They wanted a king, a capital, a centralized
government, and all that this monarchy could bring them. The
eventual consequences of this decision were ten tribes lost and
two others in a Babylonian exile. No wonder then that the
literary traditions preserved by this remnant were those that
presented emphatically the dangers of monarchy, of civilization—of the sedentary way of life itself.

Perhaps nomadism was no longer a literal option for the exiled
remnant. But the old covenant with God, a covenant for land
with the nomadic twelve tribes, had been, as Jeremiah said,
broken. The Hebrews had been given the land promised, but
had failed to resist the temptation of civilization. Now there
would be a new covenant with no connection to the land.
" 'Behold the days are coming,' says the Lord, 'when I will make
a new covenant with the house of Israel and the house of Judah,
not like the covenant I made with their fathers when I took them
by the hand to bring them out of the land of Egypt, my covenant
which they broke. . . . I will put my law within them, and I will
write it upon their hearts; and I will be their God, and they shall
be my people!"

2

Brueggemann's observations show us one way we might try to
use our interpretation of Genesis 1–11 to help us understand
other biblical passages that have customarily been treated as
patchworks. We can see if, either in part or in whole, these
passages themselves follow the same basic plot as the primeval
history.

Take, for instance, the beginning of Exodus. This in Noth's
analysis is divided into not two, but three sources. Nonetheless,
we are past the time when we have to refute specifically such
claims, especially when we find that the passage has a unifying
five-part structure, a structure with which we are by now more
than a little familiar.[4]

Exodus 1:1–2:15

A. Genealogy (1:1-7)

B. First Threat (1:8-14)

    Numerical Increase of Hebrews, Hard Labor

C. Second Threat (1:15-22)

    1. Two Midwives (1:15-21)

       The midwives are named, while Pharaoh and Moses' mother and father are not.

    2. Male infants thrown into the Nile (1:22)

D. Final Threat (2:1-10)

    Moses' "Flood," Salvation in the *tēbah*

E. Resolution (2:11-15)

    Moses goes out to Midian

Let us now look at the text:

> 1:1 These are the names of the sons of Israel who came to Egypt with Jacob, each with his household: ²Reuben, Simeon, Levi, and Judah, ³Issachar, Zebulun, and Benjamin, ⁴Dan and Naphtali, Gad and Asher. ⁵All the offspring of Jacob were seventy persons; Joseph was already in Egypt. ⁶Then Joseph died, and all his brothers, and all that generation. ⁷But the descendants of Israel were fruitul and increased greatly; they multiplied and grew exceedingly strong; so that the land was filled with them.

The creation component is reduced to a genealogy of a few generations, which provides a bridge between Genesis and Exodus, and which establishes the Hebrew population in Egypt. Soon the Hebrew population multiplies, to the great annoyance of Pharaoh, who is the Enlil figure in Exodus:

> And the descendants of Israel were fruitful and abundant,
> And multiplied and became strong very, very much,
> And the land was filled with them.

In our translation above we can hear even more clearly than in the Revised Standard Version the echo of the blessing formula of Genesis 1:28, "Be fruitful and multiply, and fill the earth," now doubly expanded. Note that the three key terms of the Genesis blessing, "to be fruitful," "to multiply," and "to fill the earth," are fully preserved here.[5] (This, by the way, is the only time these terms will be found together outside of Genesis.) The evocation of the creation is followed by the three oppressions inflicted by Pharaoh. The conflict between Pharaoh and the God of the Hebrews concerning population increase may be compared to the conflict between Enlil and Enki over the problem of overpopulation in Atrahasis.

> 1:8 Now there arose a new king over Egypt, who did not know Joseph. [9]And he said to his people, "Behold, the people of Israel are too many and too mighty for us. [10]Come, let us deal shrewdly with them, lest they multiply, and, if war befall us, they join our enemies and fight against us and escape from the land." [11]Therefore they set taskmasters over them to afflict them with heavy burdens; and they built for Pharaoh store-cities, Pithom and Raamses. [12]But the more they were oppressed, the more they multiplied and the more they spread abroad. And the Egyptians were in dread of the people of Israel. [13]So they made the people of Israel serve with rigor, [14]and made their lives bitter with hard service, in mortar and brick, and in all kinds of work in the field; in all their work they made them serve with rigor.

Pharaoh's first oppression of the Hebrews is to force upon them the hard labor of building the two cities. He, like Enlil, tries to diminish the number of people, as his speech makes clear. The God of the Hebrews, like Enki, protects the people so that Pharaoh's scheme to outwit the sons of Israel fails. The Hebrews continue to multiply.

> 1:15 Then the king of Egypt said to the Hebrew midwives, one of whom was named Shiphrah and the other Puah, [16]"When you serve as midwife to the Hebrew women, and see them upon the birthstool, if it is a son, you shall kill him; but if it is a daughter, she shall live." [17]But the midwives feared God, and did not do as the king of Egypt commanded them, but let the male children live. [18]So the king of Egypt called the midwives, and said to them, "Why have you done this, and let the male children live?" [19]The midwives said to Pharaoh, "Because the Hebrew women are not like the Egyptian women; for they are vigorous and are delivered before the midwife comes to them." [20]So God dealt well with the midwives; and the people multiplied and grew very strong. [21]And because the midwives feared God he gave them families. [22]Then Pharaoh

commanded all his people, "Every son that is born to the Hebrews you shall cast into the Nile, but you shall let every daughter live."

Pharaoh's second oppression is his attempt to kill the male babies by means of the two midwives, Shiphrah and Puah. This attempt to suppress the Hebrew overpopulation also fails because, "So God dealt well with the midwives; and the people multiplied and grew very strong" (1:20). (Note the succinct echo of the overpopulation terms of 1:17.) After this failure to diminish the population, Pharaoh resorts to still severer means: a public command to kill all Hebrew male babies.

> 2:1 Now a man from the house of Levi went and took to wife a daughter of Levi. ²The woman conceived and bore a son; and when she saw that he was a goodly child, she hid him three months. ³And when she could hide him no longer she took for him a basket made of bulrushes, and daubed it with bitumen and pitch; and she put the child in it and placed it among the reeds at the river's brink. ⁴And his sister stood at a distance, to know what would be done to him. ⁵Now the daughter of Pharaoh came down to bathe at the river, and her maidens walked beside the river; she saw the basket among the reeds and sent her maid to fetch it. ⁶When she opened it she saw the child; and lo, the babe was crying. She took pity on him and said, "This is one of the Hebrews' children." ⁷Then his sister said to Pharaoh's daughter, "Shall I go and call you a nurse from the Hebrew women to nurse the child for you?" ⁸And Pharaoh's daughter said to her, "Go." So the girl went and called the child's mother. ⁹And Pharaoh's daughter said to her, "Take this child away and nurse him for me, and I will give you your wages." So the woman took the child and nursed him. ¹⁰And the child grew, and she brought him to Pharaoh's daughter, and he became her son; and she named him Moses, for she said, "Because I drew him out of the water."

Pharaoh's third oppression is the realization of the threat in 1:22. The Hebrew male babies are being drowned but Moses' mother hides him because according to the literal Hebrew, "she saw him that he was good" (2:2). Midrash, *šᵉmôt* 1:20 reports:

> The sages say: When Moses was born the whole house became flooded with light; for here it says: and she saw him (*kî-tôb hû'*) that he was a goodly child, and elsewhere it says: And God saw the light (*kî-tôb*) that it was good.

The combination of the word "to see," $r\bar{a}'\bar{a}h$, and the phrase $k\hat{\imath}$-$t\hat{o}b$ is limited to the book of Genesis with one exception. The locution is characteristic of Genesis 1 where the same configuration of these words is repeated six times.

In the spirit of good creation, the author of Exodus 2:10 borrows the words of Genesis. When Moses' mother sees her newborn son, how good he is, she cannot help defying Pharaoh's command by hiding her son. And then when she can no longer hide him, she seeks some other way to save her son (2:2-3). The famous story of the baby Moses in the basket of bulrushes corresponds to Noah's Flood and to the Great Flood of Atrahasis. The story occupies the same relative position in Exodus 1-2 as did Noah's Flood in Genesis and the Great Flood in Atrahasis. All three stories contain the motif of salvation of a hero from the water—the last and severest of the three threats against the undesirable population.

In addition to the motif parallels between the Genesis and Exodus flood stories noted above, there are lexical-syntactical parallels that demonstrate the Moses story to be a miniature flood story. These parallels are found in the description of how Noah is to build his $t\bar{e}bah$:ark and how Moses' mother constructs the $t\bar{e}bah$:basket for her child. Noah was commanded:

Make for yourself a $t\bar{e}bah$ of gopher wood. . . . and pitch it with pitch inside and outside (Genesis 6:14).

In the book of Exodus, the actions of Moses' mother are described thus:

She took for him a $t\bar{e}bah$ of bulrushes and she pitched it with pitch and with mortar (Exodus 2:3).

These sentences from Genesis and Exodus correspond in many ways: the person is mentioned for whom the $t\bar{e}bah$ is constructed; the key word $t\bar{e}bah$ occurs in the Old Testament exclusively in these stories; the building material for the $t\bar{e}bah$ is specified in a construct chain; puns involving words for "pitch" are found in both (kpr in Genesis and hmr in Exodus); the vessel is twice sealed, "inside and outside" in Genesis and "with pitch and with mortar" in Exodus. They correspond in too many ways to be anything other than intended parallels. Moses is a second Noah.

Cassuto observed this long ago:

> The word, ark, *tēbah,* occurs only in the two sections of the Bible: here and in the section of the flood. This is certainly not a mere coincidence. By this verbal parallelism Scripture apparently intends to draw attention to the thematic analogy. In both instances one worthy of being saved and destined to bring salvation to others is to be rescued from death by drowning.[6]

Exodus continues:

> 2:11 One day, when Moses had grown up, he went out to his people and looked on their burdens; and he saw an Egyptian beating a Hebrew, one of his people. [12]He looked this way and that, and seeing no one he killed the Egyptian and hid him in the sand. [13]When he went out the next day, behold, two Hebrews were struggling together; and he said to the man that did the wrong, "Why do you strike your fellow?" [14]He answered, "Who made you a prince and a judge over us? Do you mean to kill me as you killed the Egyptian?" Then Moses was afraid, and thought, "Surely the thing is known." [15]When Pharaoh heard of it, he sought to kill Moses. But Moses fled from Pharaoh, and stayed in the land of Midian; and he sat down by a well. . . .
> [23]In the course of those many days the king of Egypt died. And the people of Israel groaned under their bondage, and cried out for help, and their cry under bondage came up to God. [24]And God heard their groaning, and God remembered his covenant with Abraham, with Isaac, and with Jacob. [25]And God saw the people of Israel, and God knew their condition.

The dispersion motif is clear enough here, but the story itself seems to have much more in common with Cain and Abel than with the Tower of Babel. Having so tightly associated the two ark stories, the author follows more loosely here. Moses kills another man; this time it is the soon-to-be nomadic Moses killing the already civilized Egyptian, rather than the soon-to-be civilized Cain killing the already nomadic Abel. And Moses, when his homicide is found out, does worry, like Cain, that others will do unto him as he has done unto another. (It is striking, by the way, how the Cain story epitomizes the hypocrisy of the founder of civilization; he thinks that human life in general is a contingent good, but he does not regard his own as such.)

Parallels also exist with the Tower of Babel story. The oppression of the Hebrews was, apart from the infanticide, the harsh labor of building of cities. (Of course we are not surprised that the building of cities is connected with the practice of infanticide.) This city-building has already been subtly connected by the author with the Tower of Babel.

Look, for instance, at the way the Pharaoh expresses himself in Exodus 1:10: "Come let us deal shrewdly with them, lest they multiply." This particular grammatical structure—*hābāh* + cohortative + "lest"—seems to occur only one other place in the whole Bible. "Let us build a city and a tower whose top is in the sky, let us make a name, lest we be scattered upon the face of the whole earth."

Moreover, in both passages there seems to be a play on the words *hēmār* ("bitumen") and *hōmer* ("mortar"). A literal translation of Genesis 11:3 shows the futility of their activity being underlined by a repetitiveness culminated in the paronomasia between *hēmār* and *hōmer*.

"Habah, let us brick bricks,
Let us burn them burningly;"
So they had brick for stone,
Bitumen (*hēmar*) had they for mortar (*hōmer*).

In Exodus 1:14 this is now replaced with a fine specimen of climactic cacophony to stress the severity of the slavery with the seven-fold repetition of the preposition *b:in*.

And they embittered their lives,
In severe slavery,
In bitumen and in mortar
In all the slavery in the field,
With all the slaveries,
In which they enslaved them in vexation (1:14).

We can summarize our findings about Exodus 1–11 most effectively in a chart (page 118). We will add for the sake of completeness Matthew 1–3, since its connection with Exodus 1–2 has long been noted.[7]

	ATRAHASIS	GENESIS 1–11	EXODUS 1–2	MATTHEW 1–3
A.	Creation of Man (Tab I. 1-248) Summary of Work of Gods Creation of Man	(Gen. 1:1–2:25) Sum of Work of God Creation of Man	(Exod. 1:1-7) A Genealogy	(Matt. 1:1-17) A Genealogy
B.	Man's Numerical Increase (I. 249-415) Attempt to Decrease Numbers Threat of Death by Plague	(2:4–3:24) Adam and Eve Near Death	(1:8-14) Hard Labor of Hebrews	(1:18-25) Joseph and Mary "Virgin Birth"
C.	Second Attempt to Decrease: Double Story (II. i. 1–vi. 55) 1. Threat of Death: Drought 2. Severer Means	(4:1–5:32) 1. Cain and Abel 2. Lamech's Taunt	(1:15-22) 1. Two Midwives 2. Severer Means	(2:1-18) 1. 3 Wise Men 2. Infanticide
D.	Final Solution (II. vii.–III. vi. 40) Atrahasis' Flood Salvation in Boat	(6:1–9:7) Noah's Flood Salvation in tēbah	(2:1-10) Moses and the Nile Salvation in tēbah	(2:19-23) Flight to Egypt Exodus Motif
E.	Resolution (III. vi. 41–viii. 18) Compromise between Enlil and Enki "Birth Control"	(9:8–11:32) Dispersion—Abram leaves Ur Exodus Motif	(2:11-25) Moses goes out to Midian Exodus Motif	(3:1-17) Baptism of John River Jordan Flood Motif: Dove

3

What is particularly suggestive in the results of the last section is that we have seen a shorter section replicating the organization of a much larger section. If Genesis 1–11 shares its structure with a much smaller unit such as Exodus 1–2, could it also share its structure with a much larger unit?

Ivan Ball has argued with considerable persuasiveness that the whole organization of Zephaniah can be found in miniature in one part.[8] Could the organization of Genesis as a whole be itself replicated in Genesis 1–11? The following chart suggests how this might be so.[9]

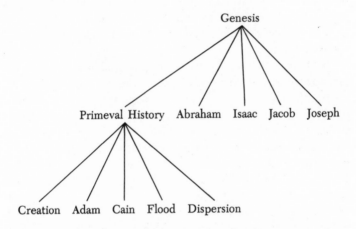

If this interpretation is correct, the repetition which we found in the Adam, Cain, and Flood stories would also be found in the larger Abraham, Isaac, and Jacob narratives. In fact, parallels in the stories of these three patriarchs are not hard to find. The wives of these three patriarchs are all imported from Mesopotamia, the land of patriarchal origin. All three wives are barren and require divine intervention to realize the covenant of Abraham, the father of a multitude of nations. This triple barrenness of the wives strikingly parallels at the familial level the three-fold extinction threat to the species, which we saw as characteristic of the middle three stories of the primeval history.

There are two obvious difficulties with this interpretation. First, it requires that the brief Isaac section be treated as a full-fledged patriarchal narrative, rather than as the simple connector it seems. But we have already seen in our analysis of the Tower of Babel story that a brief story can be of stunning complexity. Second, our interpretation requires that the Joseph narrative be taken as separate from the other patriarchal narratives.

This second difficulty is easily resolved when we realize that the Joseph narrative upon closer examination does seem very different from the others. Wives and barrenness are not important. And as Johannan Muffs argues, Abraham, Isaac, and Jacob are all presented as noble warriors, but Joseph is far from a noble warrior.[10] The main setting of the patriarchal stories is the Canaan of nomads; the main setting of the Joseph story is civilized Egypt.

The Joseph story, in our interpretation, should not only be separated from the other patriarchal narratives; it should parallel the primeval history of Genesis 1–11 much as the Tower of Babel paralleled the creation of Genesis 1:1–2:3. There are some verbal indications of this. The phrase, *rûah 'elōhîm: the wind/spirit of God*, which is used in the story of creation to help express the primordial condition of the earth—"And the earth was *tōhû wābōhû* and the *rûah 'elōhîm* was hovering over the face of the waters"—is found in the Joseph cycle in a speech of Pharaoh extolling Joseph's wisdom and ability in 41:37. "And Pharaoh said to his servants, 'Can we find a man like this in whom is the *rûah 'elōhîm?*'" Another verbal parallel is a formulaic expression, namely a verb of seeing in combination with *kî tôb: that it was good*. This formula is repeated impressively six times in the first chapter, then it is used ironically two more times in the primeval history—once in the story of Adam and Eve, "And the woman saw *kî tôb: how good* the tree for food . . . and she took of its fruit and she ate" (3:6) and again in, "The sons of God saw the daughters of men *kî tôb: how good* they were" (6:2).

We must then jump to the Joseph cycle to see this formulaic expression used again. There it occurs twice: the first time in the narrative of the dreams of the butler and the baker, "And the chief baker saw *how good: kî tôb* the interpretation, he said to Joseph, 'I also had a dream . . . ' " (40:16) and for the second time in the Blessing of Jacob in the passage dealing with Issachar, "He saw the resting place *kî tôb: how good* it was" (49:15).

If this analysis of hierarchical structure in Genesis is plausible, we should not only expect specific parallels between the Joseph narrative and the primeval history considered as a whole. We should also expect that the Joseph story as the conclusion of Genesis would have specific parallels with the Tower of Babel story as the conclusion of the Genesis primeval history. And at a general level there is a striking parallel, or at least contrast. The Tower of Babel story, as we have interpreted it in light of its ancient Near Eastern parallels, tells how God thwarted men's civilizing efforts in order that they fufill their destiny to multiply. The Joseph story tells how God forced one family to give up its nomadic life (and move to a civilized center) in order that his promise to preserve its life and make it flourish be fulfilled. There exists, therefore, an apparent tension between these two stories, a tension which belies a deeper unity. Both have the theme of dispersion or exodus; both speak of a radical change in the form of life. And if we put the last stage of the post-Babel genealogy next to the last verse of Genesis itself, we find these similarities forcefully present:

11:27 Now these are the descendants of Terah. Terah was the father of Abram, Nahor, and Haran; and Haran was the father of Lot. ²⁸Haran died before his father Terah in the land of his birth, in Ur of the Chaldeans. ²⁹And Abram and Nahor took wives; the name of Abram's wife was Sarai, and the name of Nahor's wife, Milcah, the daughter of Haran the father of Milcah and Iscah. ³⁰Now Sarai was barren; she had no child.
³¹Terah took Abram his son and Lot the son of Haran, his grandson, and Sarai his daughter-in-law, his son Abram's

50:24 And Joseph said to his brothers, "I am about to die; but God will visit you, and bring you up out of this land to the land which he swore to Abraham, to Isaac, and to Jacob." ²⁵Then Joseph took an oath of the sons of Israel, saying, "God will visit you, and you shall carry up my bones from here." ²⁶So Joseph died, being a hundred and ten years old; and they embalmed him, and he was put in a coffin in Egypt.

121

wife, and they went forth together from Ur of the Chaldeans
to go into the land of Canaan; but
when they came to Haran, they
settled there. ³²The days of
Terah were two hundred and
five years; and Terah died in
Haran.

In both stories we have a specific mention of Abram, in both a
death, in both a hopeful reference to entrance into the Promised
Land, and both look forward to the yet unfinished business that
lies ahead. And perhaps most important, both these deaths—the
death of Joseph and the death of Terah—are the narrative
preliminaries of a divinely ordained exodus: Abram and his
family from Haran, and Moses and his people from Egypt.

This last statement, which treats the Joseph narrative as a
preliminary for that of Moses, might seem provocative. It is
intended to be provocative. If Genesis 1–11 has a five-part
structure, and if Genesis as a whole has a five-part structure that
loosely parallels it, then the question naturally arises as to the
relevance of this structure to that most famous five-part work, the
Pentateuch itself. If there is a hierarchical structure, could it
have three levels?

If it has three levels, then we can expect Genesis and
Deuteronomy to end on a similar note (much as we found the
primeval history and Genesis as a whole ending on comparable
notes). Genesis, of course, ends with Joseph's peaceful death, and
yet it is a death which points to the coming of radical change, and
recalls the unfulfilled promise to Abraham for land. Joseph himself
says, "God will visit you, and you shall carry my bones from here."
Deuteronomy ends with the death of Moses and with the Hebrew
people on the verge of their move into the Promised Land.[11]

We would also expect the middle three books to be thematically
repetitive. And these three are what we might call wilderness
books—books that describe how the Hebrew people survived the
threats to extinction as they came out of Egypt and went toward the
Promised Land. (Perhaps it is not too trivial to note that these three
books begin with the conjunction *w*: "and," whereas Genesis and
Deuteronomy do not.) And while the middle three books are

concerned with the telling of this long Exodus story, the instructions found in Deuteronomy are presented as a speech given by Moses, a *re*telling of the Exodus. And, of course, the less formalized divine instructions in Genesis come to be understood as a *fore*telling of the Exodus.

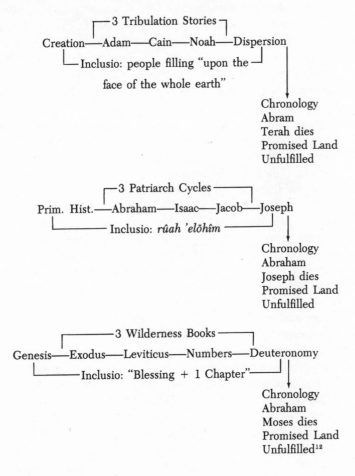

4

We have shown that the five-part structure of Genesis 1–11 is shared by some other sections of the Hebrew Bible. We have shown that it can be shared by units both smaller and larger—and perhaps that sometimes it will be shared only partially. We have seen the ways this structure has been adapted to serve different functions, much as the author of Genesis 1–11 adapts the Atrahasis structure for his own purposes. We do not know if a further examination of the narrative of the early reign of David will produce a parallel to the creation section of Genesis. Neither do we know if the broadly suggestive outline of the Pentateuch will prove to be anything more than an aperçu. However, biblical scholars should expect to find other sections where the Atrahasis structure is repeated. Doubtless there are numerous places where this occurs and some probably have a subtlety that rivals Genesis 1–11. To take one example, the Book of Jonah—that consummate masterpiece of Hebrew irony—seems to use our five-part structure, but in the opposite order.[13] It is as if the wise author of Jonah has stood Genesis on its head to make us laugh while we learn from his wisdom.

The five-part Atrahasis structure is a crucial inheritance of the Hebrew tradition from the ancient Near Eastern civilizations. In a more general sense we have shown that at least one Hebrew author—and a most important one at that—has assumed on the part of the audience a knowledge of this convention. We have seen how, when we recovered the convention, enigmas in Genesis 1–11 (which perplexed our interpreters for millennia) disappear with breathtaking swiftness. For example, our interpretation of the Garden of Eden story takes but a page.

Perhaps the Atrahasis structure is the most important convention that the Hebrew tradition received from ancient Near Eastern civilizations. Just perhaps. Nonetheless, it can scarcely be the only one. There must be any number of conventions—of genres, if you prefer—which govern portions of the Hebrew Bible, and which the Hebrew author sets his message against. We have reconstructed just one portion of the total rhetorical heritage. We have no doubt that many other portions can be found in ancient Near Eastern texts long known and translated, waiting for someone looking with a literary eye to see them. We need more people to look for rhetoric, for genre, for convention—not primarily for documentary traditions.

But there are still more important implications of what we have done. We offer a persuasive refutation of the documentary analysis of Genesis 1–11. The best defense of this hypothesis now becomes its analyses of other portions of the Hebrew Bible. And, of course, as a dominant research paradigm of biblical scholarship for an entire century, this hypothesis has produced its documentary interpretation of virtually every major book of the Bible. Editors and redactors are everywhere, each book with its own complex geological strata. If our refutation is persuasive, then much of this work will have to be reconsidered. We must go back through the same materials, at once building on the observations of documentary analysts and seeking more sophisticated unities than those analysts were willing to entertain. Such analysis will take a very long time, just as an application of the documentary hypothesis to the whole Bible took generations. How far unitary analysis will advance, how far documentary analysis will recede, is impossible to predict. And perhaps in the end we will only be confronting our own ignorance, a Kantian antinomy of pure reason.

One thing, if anything, we are certain of: the documentary hypothesis at present is woefully overextended. Jowett once said that the most difficult thing to learn is how to deal with unequal conditions of knowledge. When we look at the table of Pentateuchal traditions appended to Noth's *History of Penta-teuchal Traditions*, we do not have to learn this most difficult lesson. We have all the delusive comfort of an epistemologically closed world in which scholars can while away their lives worrying about the attribution of this or that half-verse. Think of the table of chemical elements in the late nineteenth century, just before radioactivity blew it away with the kind of transmutations the Renaissance alchemists had sought.

Notes / Chapter V

1. Martin Noth, *Pentateuchal Traditions*, p. 2.
2. Walter Brueggemann, "David and His Theologian," *CBQ* 30 (1968):156-81. There is, by the way, a slight echo of the creation account vocabulary when in II Samuel 11:2 David sees how good Bathsheba is to look upon.
3. Hayden White, *Metahistory* (Baltimore: Johns Hopkins University Press, 1973). His treatment of myths is dependent upon Northrop Frye, *Anatomy of Criticism: Four Essays* (Princeton: Princeton University Press, 1954).

4. Our interpretation of Exodus 1-2 was first presented by Kikawada to the Society of Biblical Literature in Chicago, 1973. A version of this interpretation can be found in James Ackerman, "The Literary Context of the Moses Birth Story," *Literary Interpretations of Biblical Narratives* (Nashville: Abingdon Press, 1974), pp. 74-119. For a documentary interpretation see Martin Noth, *Exodus* (Philadelphia: Westminster Press, 1962). For further examination of ancient Near Eastern elements in the story, see B. S. Childs, "The Birth of Moses," *JBL* 84 (1965):109-22.

5. Pointed out by S. R. Driver, *Exodus* (Cambridge: Cambridge University Press, 1953), p. 2.

6. Umberto Cassuto, *A Commentary on the Book of Exodus* (Jerusalem: Magnes, 1967), pp. 18-19.

7. For a comprehensive treatment of Matthew 1-3, see Raymond Brown, *The Birth of the Messiah* (New York: Doubleday, 1977).

8. Ivan J. Ball, *A Rhetorical Study of Zephaniah* (Diss., Graduate Theological Union, 1972).

9. We have found Bruce Dahlberg, "On Recognizing the Unity of Genesis," *Theology Digest* 24 (1976):360-67 a particularly stimulating discussion of the unity of Genesis. For the subsequent observations on the patriarchal wives, we are indebted to Mary Streitwieser.

10. J. Muffs, "Abraham the Noble Warrior," *Abstracts: Sixth World Congress of Jewish Studies* (Jerusalem, 1973).

11. The connection between these two conclusions was observed independently by D. J. A. Clines, *The Theme of the Pentateuch* (Sheffield: University Press, 1978), p. 25.

12. We might note that the covenant of these three levels are progressively more specific. The rainbow covenant is for all living things; Abraham's covenant is for the nations that will spring from him; Moses' covenant is for the Hebrews alone. This pattern has been convincingly observed by Frank Cross, *Canaanite Myth and Hebrew Epic* (Cambridge: Harvard University Press, 1973).

13. See Isaac Kikawada and Eric Hesse, "Jonah and Genesis 11-1," *Annual of Japanese Biblical Institute*, vol. 10 (1984), forthcoming.

EPILOGUE

·

We would be remiss if we did not raise one final issue. The documentary analysis of the Bible, whether intentionally or not, has gone hand-in-hand historically with an ethical condescension to, or even rejection of, the Bible. The documentary analysts conclude that the Bible is literarily primitive; cultural critics conclude that it is morally backward as well.

To our mind this ethical anti-Semitism has received its most forceful formulation since Nietzsche in Simone Weil's profound and justly famous essay on *The Iliad*. There she contrasts the humanity of the Greeks with the chauvinism of the Hebrews. She groups the Hebrews with the murderous Romans as peoples who "believed themselves exempt from the common misery of man" and who therefore treated their "vanquished as an abomination." She adds, "The Romans and Hebrews have been admired, read, imitated in actions and in words, cited every time there was need to justify a crime through 20 centuries of Christianity."[1]

What we wish to do in this epilogue is to show how our general approach to reading the Bible can provide a response to challenges like Weil's. We want to show how rejecting the literary primitivism of the Bible helps one respond to those who argue for its moral backwardness. We have, for instance, shown that Genesis 1–11 should not be condescended to aesthetically, for its author plays subtly and ironically with a distant, older epic of his civilization, much as James Joyce plays with Homer. Note how this reading of Genesis 1–11 provides, almost by the way, a

127

response to Weil. The author of Genesis 1–11 is willing—indeed, seems to be insisting—that we reject civilization and all its works rather than be implicated in the crimes that are necessary to its foundation and continuance. Perhaps no primeval history of the ancient world stands in starker contrast to Genesis 1–11 than the sentimental epic of Virgil in which pious Aeneas sadly commits every betrayal and crime necessary to become the founder of eternal Rome.[2]

Of course, for us to focus on Genesis 1–11 is not a fair test. It was a fair test for the documentary hypothesis since it seemed to provide the strongest evidence for it. Weil, however, would find her strongest evidence in those books which actually describe the conquests of the Hebrews. And of these books perhaps the hardest for us would be the Book of Judges. In this book more than in any other within the Hebrew canon (with the possible exception of Esther) we find Hebrew heroes exulting in their treatment of the vanquished as an abomination, the chosen of God boasting of their own brutality.

We must ask if the author of Judges intends for us to respond by sharing in this boasting. But even in this question there is to be found an added difficulty, for us a welcome difficulty. The Book of Judges is commonly regarded as literarily primitive, a hodgepodge of heroic tales, two of which themselves—the Deborah and Samson stories—are rough patchworks. Or so the epigones of Wellhausen, von Rad, and Noth assure us.[3] To answer Weil we must answer them as well. And our answer is that Judges is both literarily sophisticated and ethically admirable.

Let us return to the question of how we are intended to respond. In some instances the response intended by a passage in Judges is not difficult to guess. How, for instance, should the reader respond to the following verse from the episode of Ehud?

And Ehud reached with his left hand, took the sword from his right thigh, and thrust it into his belly; and the hilt also went in after the blade, and the fat closed over the blade, for he did not draw the sword out of his belly (3:21-22).

Whatever a reader's feelings about killing an unarmed person with a concealed weapon (or, for that matter, about people who normally use their sinister hand), the detail of the fat closing over the blade cannot help but provoke our disgust. And surely that disgust increases if, with the Authorized Version, we follow the Targum and Vulgate by adding: "the dirt came out." The excrement oozing from the fat does more for us than simply specify that the knife had entered the king's colon. It shapes our response to that event.

And our response to this verse is, we think, typical of that hoped for by Judges as a whole. And an extraordinary response it is. At the very moment we might expect the author to allow us to exult over God's deliverance of his people, he dwells instead on disgusting details. This is no racial melodrama; the author will not pander to our ethnic prejudices.

Of course, sections of Judges do exult in God's deliverance— Judges indeed contains the most famous of such exultations, the song of Deborah. But let us look at this song in its context.

The very death of Sisera, as described in the prose version, is disturbing. Sisera is killed by Jael, with whom he sought sanctuary as the wife of an ally. She deceives this suppliant by the generosity of her welcome. She goes out to meet him, and soothes him: "Have no fear." When he asks for water, she gives him milk. Then, exhausted in his defeat, Sisera, trusting in the treaty, her hospitality, her obvious concern, falls asleep. "Jael the wife of Heber took a tent peg, and took a hammer in her hand, and went softly to him and drove the peg into his temple till it went down into the ground, as he was lying fast asleep from weariness" (4:21).

Why add the detail "till it went down into the ground" unless to emphasize the brutality of the act? And why then add the clause "as he was lying fast asleep from weariness" unless to excite our sympathy for him? However despicable Sisera was as a person, his vulnerability at this moment—defeated, deceived, exhausted, asleep—cannot help but excite our compassion. Twentieth-century commentators recognize this and also recognize that our horror at this murder would have been shared by an ancient audience. The Tyndale Biblical Commentary on Judges admits that Jael "broke every accepted standard of hospitality."[4] Soggin, in a similar vein, after examining various attempts to explain away Jael's culpability, finally admits that despite them "the scene remains sinister . . . it cannot but raise negative reactions, in the same way as the classical parallels mentioned above caused their audience to shudder." Nonetheless, having reached this conclusion, Soggin will not take the next obvious step and admit that perhaps the author of Judges was a master of his material, wanting us to shudder. Rather, Soggin explains the effect as a flaw resulting from the fact that the story of Jael was "probably too deeply rooted in the tradition" to be ignored; the author (or editor) "preferred the risk of repeating it to the risk of leaving it out."[5]

This would be a plausible argument if the Jael story were an isolated horror. But the Book of Judges leads us from one horror to another. And not the least of these horrors is the song of Deborah.

The most striking aspect of Deborah's account of the murder of Sisera is its repeated inaccuracy. Of course, we can assume *a priori* that any inconsistencies between the prose and the poetic accounts are the result of two inconsistent traditions being uncritically combined by an editor with much respect for tradition and little literary taste. Why, however, make such an assumption if accepting the inconsistencies as intended both increases the power of the work and is in keeping with responses that the narrative has already evoked? Let us assume that the author of Judges was a master of what he surveyed. Then we can see that the author intended the inaccuracies as he intended the shudders—these particular inaccuracies are there, in fact, to make us shudder once again.

> Most blessed of women be Jael,
>   the wife of Heber the Kenite,
>   of tent-dwelling women most blessed.
> He asked water and she gave him milk,
>   she brought him curds in a lordly bowl.
> She put her hand to the tent peg
>   and her right hand to the workmen's mallet;
> she struck Sisera a blow,
>   she crushed his head,
>   she shattered and pierced his temple.
> He sank, he fell,
>   he lay still at her feet;
> at her feet he sank, he fell;
>   where he sank, there he fell dead (5:24-27).

Deborah sings that "he asked water and she gave him milk." Yes, that was the way it was earlier reported. "She brought him curds in a lordly bowl." No; the earlier version specifies that Jael gave him milk from a skin. "She struck Sisera . . . pierced his temple." Yes. "She crushed his head . . . shattered [it]." Not quite; she might have done that if she had hit him indiscriminately with a blunt instrument like a mallet—but rather she nailed him with a peg to the floor. The crushing and shattering, like the cream and the dish, are details added by Deborah; the reader is uneasy about both the deception and the gore, and yet Deborah is adding details that only increase our unease. She certainly is not responding to this event as we are. She so relishes this homicide that she cannot restrict herself to the truth. And hence even her own embellished version of shattering the exhausted and sleeping Sisera's skull is not enough for her. "He sank, he fell, he lay still at her feet; at her feet he sank, he fell; where he sank, there he fell dead" (5:25-27).

We perhaps should not be picky at an exciting moment like this, but Sisera did not fall down dead. He was alseep on the ground when he died. Here Deborah is not only being inconsistent with the first version; she is even contradicting herself. The Cambridge Biblical Commentary admits as much and explains it by hypothesizing that these verses "may, therefore, represent two variant traditions regarding the death of Sisera, only one of which is reproduced in the prose narrative."[6] Now it is not just the editor who in putting the prose and poetic versions together cannot make up his mind between two contrary traditions; now it is also whoever wrote the Song of Deborah itself. What has been lost sight of (or rather sound of) in such scholastic interpolations is that the speaker of the poem has gradually been working herself up into a state of exultant frenzy over an act of barbarism. The fact that she is not telling us a story exactly like the one we have already heard, that she cannot even keep her own story straight, is the author's way of telling us that she is not what Booth would call a "reliable narrator."[7] She is unreliable as a source for the details of the story and unreliable as a guide to how we should be responding to it. Her inaccuracies and internal inconsistencies are the author's way of subtly telling us that her responses are not his—nor should they be ours.

The author does not want us to think that perhaps Sisera had his skull bashed in with a mallet while he was standing. Nor does he expect that we will be charmed by Deborah's need to have Sisera fall in mortal agony again and again (like a movie director showing a particularly satisfying piece of gore in loving slow motion over and over). How could he have put more emotional distance between us and his creature than have her move away from the corpse of Sisera to his mother's understandable worries and the mistaken reassurances she receives? Who cannot feel sympathy with the mother or revulsion at the inhuman monster Deborah?

> Out of the window she peered,
>> the mother of Sisera gazed through the lattice:
> "Why is his chariot so long in coming?
>> Why tarry the hoofbeats of chariots?"
> Her wisest ladies make answer,
>> nay, she gives answer to herself,
> "Are they not finding and dividing the spoil?—
>> A maiden or two for every man;
> spoil of dyed stuffs for Sisera,
>> spoil of dyed stuffs embroidered,
>> two pieces of dyed work embroidered for my neck
>> as spoil?" (5:28-30)

Notice how Deborah in her excitement keeps correcting herself to make the story better. First the mother's ladies, the wisest of them, are to reassure her that her son is all right—make them be the wisest so that the mother reasonably will believe them and that will make her grief even greater when the news comes. No, the mother could then blame her ladies for misleading her. Do not distract from the mother. Let her reassure herself. Indeed, let her start to imagine all her son will be bringing with him. What does she most want in her imaginative celebration of his victory? Dyed stuff, dyed stuff embroidered, two pieces of dyed stuff embroidered for her neck. As Deborah rants about the dyed stuff, she finally loses patience with her own imaginary story of how Sisera's mother learns that her son has been killed ignominiously. In what is perhaps the most remarkable anacoluthon in the whole Bible, Deborah suddenly drops her story and bursts out in exaltation.

So perish all thine enemies, O Lord!
But thy friends be like the sun as he rises in his might.

And the land had rest for forty years (5:31).

The shift from the shrieking of Deborah to the detachment of the narrator could not be more striking. And we know perfectly well that a peace based on such frenzy will scarcely last. Indeed the very next verse begins the narrative of another fall. "The people of Israel did what was evil in the sight of the Lord" (6:1).

Does no modern commentator sympathize with Sisera's mother? Gerelman, for one, does sympathize with her, although he is not at all sure that he should. He sees a remarkable contrast between Deborah's treatment of the mother of Sisera and Aeschylus' treatment of the mother of Xerxes in *The Persians*. He can only conclude, "In Greek tragedy, however, the manner of considering the enemies is quite different from that in the Hebrew song. Aeschylus is a patriot, but no chauvinist."[8] Are we to identify the author of Judges with the barbarism of Deborah? If so, then we must concede that Weil in her harshest judgments of the Hebrews cannot be disputed on the basis of this text.[9] To avoid this conclusion, to separate the author of Judges from the voice of Deborah (and the duplicity of Jael), we need only believe that the author of Judges is capable of irony and of sharing in our humanity.

But why employ irony, why invite disgust when describing the heroes of Judges? The author's attitude toward them is surely not the attitude he takes toward God's repeated deliverance of his people. This repeated deliverance would indeed be the cause of joy and exultation. But this is only one-half of the story—and the response of the reader is tied to the other half. The author's attitude toward these heroes is rather the attitude he thinks his readers should have toward the repeated *need* for God to save (and to punish) his people, to do so again and again long after he has already brought them to the promised land. Embarrassment, revulsion, disgust. God might well have been saving the sinful Israelites, but he was sending them exactly the kind of judges they deserved, judges who embodied the Hebrews' own weakness and perversity.

The Book of Judges, therefore, can be seen as a moral test for its readers. Those who are like the sinning Israelites will simply enjoy the story of Deborah as a victory of "us" over "them"—and will be indifferent to the truth or to the sentiments of common humanity, as long as this indifference is to "our" advantage. Those, in contrast, who do see the ironies, see the parallel between the mother of Sisera and the daughter of Jephthah, the treachery of Jael and that of Delilah, will find Judges an excruciating experience, a wrenching call to humility and repentance.

If this interpretation holds, then we are now in a position to understand the most important (and perplexing) story of Judges. Samson fits the pattern of a champion worthy of a people unworthy of their God—a champion strong but stupid, willful, lustful, unclean; one of his great triumphs coming after the humiliation of Judah (the once vaunted lion's whelp) and through the ridiculous agency of the ass's jawbone; his other triumph coming after his own humiliation by the uncircumcised and through an act tantamount to suicide. Even in this final triumph the author takes care to deflect our sympathies. Samson calls not for God's glory but for his own revenge. And then there is the young boy who places Samson's hands on the pillars, the young boy who in an act of kindness places Samson so he can rest, a young boy who for his kindness will be crushed to death.

We need not now, given this perspective, worry—as many commentators have—about the fairness of the riddle Samson asked the Philistines (a riddle we quote in a more literal translation than the RSV):

> Out of the eater came forth food
> Out of the strong came forth sweet (14:14).

It is unfair because it is based on private experience, not the commonplace ingeniously disguised. That he should have behaved so unfairly is in keeping with Samson's character. He certainly does not behave noticeably better than the Philistines in the story—if anything, worse. But we can do more with the riddle than that.

We can also now entertain with sympathy the suggestions of some critics that Samson's answer is wrong.[10] In particular, we can now understand the importance of the suggestion made by Torczyner in the 1920s that the correct solution to this riddle is "vomit."[11] That this riddle should have these two answers is a masterstroke of irony. From Samson's point of view the answer is entirely private and denotes an act of heroism; from the universal point of view, in contrast, it denotes an object of disgust. Here is the epitome of the dark wisdom of Judges: the heroism of Samson is the vomit of God.

But the irony cuts even deeper. The Philistines give the answer to the riddle: "What is sweeter than honey? What is stronger than a lion?" It has been often observed that this does itself seem to share the form of a riddle. If it is a riddle, then the answer is obvious enough, at least to the reader of the Samson story. Samson is stronger than the lion; he killed it. The death of Philistines will be sweeter than honey to him once he learns that they have ploughed with his heifer. Their answer contains within it the unforeseen consequence of their success.

The Cambridge Biblical Commentary almost sees this point: "To the Philistines 'the strong' might have been thought to refer to Samson's virility and sexual prowess." But it backs away from the response, unable to concede the author of Judges the capacity for dramatic irony: "In the event this was a false clue, a red herring."[12] In the event this was a true clue, but for the reader, not for the Philistines.

Such clues to the future can be found elsewhere in the Samson story once we begin to look. Take, for instance, the actual episode on which the Samson riddle is supposedly based: the pulling of honey from the carcass of the young lion Samson killed. Obviously this episode is thematically appropriate in a number of respects. For instance, Samson's willingness to defile himself for sweets is a nice commentary on his desire for Gentile women. And the juxtaposition of an object of desire and an object of disgust is in keeping with the general view of history. We might even think we find a resonance with Deborah, for is not her name etymologically associated with the honey bee?[13]

But why a young lion? Certainly a hero as great as Samson could have killed one fully grown. Is there a justification of this particular detail elsewhere in the story? A young lion, we would suggest, because the tribe of Judah is associated with it. In this story the lion's whelp are the cowardly collaborators who turn Samson over to the Philistines after he seeks refuge with them. They, the carcass of their old selves, betray him, but from this betrayal he draws the honeyed victory. The episode of the young lion is itself a riddle to which the later episode is the answer.

Once we begin to work in this direction the surface of the Samson story shimmers, takes on an almost surreal character. This is what is to be expected, according to Booth's *Rhetoric of Irony,* when irony reaches to the marrow of a story.[14] But before we allow Samson to dissolve into enigmatic nothingness, we should perhaps give this reading of Samson, and Judges as a whole, one last test.

Chapter 16 has long been regarded as a problematic conclusion to the Samson story. *The Jerome Biblical Commentary* expresses the problem, with a typical solution:

> The existence of two endings to the saga of Samson in 15:20 and 16:31, and the fact that the narrative in Jgs. 16 is the least edifying of the entire complex, would point to the conclusion that . . . the first redactor had omitted Jgs. 16 as irrelevant to his own theological message and terminated the narrative with 15:20; then the second editor replaced it together with his own ending in 16:31.[15]

The Anchor Bible goes even further; in dividing the Book of Judges into four parts it locates the division between parts two and three at the end of chapter 15—the entire Samson story is not even in the same part of the book.[16] Even the most ambitious attempt to retain the unity of the Samson story, that of Crenshaw, admits that 15:20 is an intrusion, a "redactional comment."[17] We, however, believe that not only do 15 and 16 fit together and are the work of one author, an author of considerable subtlety and skill, but also that even the so-called "redactional comment" contributes to this unity.

All this becomes clear once we ask the question: Why does the author have Samson kill the Philistines with the jawbone of an ass? Of course, we have to ask that question knowing that this is more than just a detail of tradition and a key to the place name—it is a clue. If we look for an ass in the Samson story, a strong, stupid, recalcitrant beast of burden, we do not have to look any further than Samson himself. And this connection is underlined in chapter 16 where we find Samson both carrying around the doors of a city and also using his renewed strength to grind the grain. And why the *jawbone* of the ass? Samson does talk too much around his women, especially in 16 when talking to Delilah leads to his downfall and then also to that of the Philistines.

Samson's boast after slaying the Philistines—"With the jawbone of an ass, heaps upon heaps / with the jawbone of an ass have I slain a thousand men."—would be the boast of God at the end of 16. Even the "heaps upon heaps" suggests the collapsed amphitheatre. Samson's boast at the end of 15 is, therefore, a riddle to which 16 is the answer. To the defeated Philistines God might say: "If you had not ploughed with my heifer, you would never have guessed my riddle." That these two episodes are to be viewed as strictly parallel is further signalled by the author's placing, at the end of each, like editorial comments: "And he judged Israel in the days of the Philistines for twenty years" (15:20). "He had been judge in Israel for twenty years" (16:31). The author prefers these two parallel twenties rather than the single forty with which he usually concludes.

One final problem. The redactor's comment in 15:20 does not immediately follow Samson's boast. The intermediary episode about Samson's thirst must also mirror his later triumph. "And he was very thirsty; and he called on the Lord and said, 'Thou hast granted this great deliverance by the hand of thy servant; and shall I now die of thirst and fall into the hands of the uncircumcised?' " For God to do a great work by your hand you will have to fall into the hands of the uncircumcised. (At their ill-fated celebration the Philistines will rejoice: "Our God has given Samson into our hand.") And you will die of your thirst, or rather in the quenching of it. "That I may be avenged upon the Philistines," you will pray in the hollow of their stadium; " . . . Let me die with the Philistines." "God split open the hollow place . . . and there came water from it. . . . And when he drank, his spirit returned and he revived." Through his death.

God withheld from this Hebrew hero the mark of Cain to protect him. The return of Samson's homicidal vigor means his own death. And this was all as it should have been.

> Out of the eater came forth food,
> Out of the strong came forth sweet (14:14).

Notes / Epilogue

1. Simone Weil, "The Iliad: A Poem of Force," *Intimations of Christianity Among the Ancient Greeks* (London: Routledge & Kegan Paul, 1957), p. 54.

2. We are perhaps being unfair to Virgil. See, for instance, W. R. Johnson, *Darkness Visible* (Berkeley: University of California Press, 1976). We are not being unfair to apologists of this empire; see Arthur Quinn, "Meditating Tacitus," *QJS* 70 (1984):53-68.

3. An extreme case of this documentary analysis of Judges is C. A. Simpson, *Composition of the Book of Judges* (Oxford: Oxford University Press, 1957). If we count up right, he requires ten documents, recensions, or editions. This makes Judges only slightly more complicated a text than *Finnegans Wake*.

4. Arthur Cundall, *Judges* (London: Tyndale, 1968), p. 100. See also Anne Kilmer, "How Was Queen Ereshkigal Fooled," *Ugarit-Forschungen* 3 (1971), 299-309.

5. J. A. Soggin, *Judges* (Philadelphia: Westminster Press, 1981), p. 78.

6. James Martin, *The Book of Judges* (Cambridge: Cambridge University Press, 1975), p. 75.

7. Wayne Booth, *The Rhetoric of Fiction* (Chicago: University of Chicago Press, 1961), pp. 211-40.

8. Gillis Gerelman, "The Song of Deborah in the Light of Stylistics," *VT* 1 (1951):173.

9. Weil, "Poem of Force."

10. This is explored in J. R. Porter, "Samson's Riddle," *JTS*, Ns. 15 (1967):106-9, in which he concludes: "It is best not to attempt the desperate task of harmonizing perfectly the episode of the lion slaying with that of finding honey, but to regard the latter as a subsequent explanation of Samson's riddle when . . . its original meaning could no longer be glimpsed."

11. Harry Torczyner, "The Riddle in the Bible," *HUCA* 1 (1924):125.

12. Martin, *Judges*, p. 166.

13. Noted, for instance, by Robert Boling, *Judges* (New York: Doubleday, 1975), p. 230.

14. Wayne Booth, *The Rhetoric of Irony* (Chicago: University of Chicago Press, 1974).

15. J. D. Crossman, "Judges," *Jerome Biblical Commentary* (Englewood Cliffs, N.J.: Prentice Hall, 1968), p. 158.

16. Boling, *Judges*, pp. 29-38.

17. James Crenshaw, "The Samson Saga," *ZAW* 86 (1974):470-503. See also his *Samson* (Atlanta: Mercer University Press, 1978), especially chap. 3.

BIBLIOGRAPHY

•

Ackerman, James. "The Literary Context of the Moses Birth Story." In *Literary Interpretations of Biblical Narratives*. Ed. K. R. R. Gros Louis, et al. Nashville: Abingdon Press, 1974.

Albright, William F. "The Location of the Garden of Eden." *AJSL* 39 (1922):15-31.

Allen, Thomas W., ed. *Homeri Opera*, v. 5. Oxford: Oxford University Press, 1919.

Alter, Robert. *The Art of Biblical Narrative*. New York: Basic Books, 1981.

Andersen, Francis I. *The Sentence in Biblical Hebrew*. The Hague: Mouton, 1974.

Anderson, B. W. "From Analysis of Synthesis: The Interpretation of Genesis 1-11." *JBL* 97 (1978):23-29.

Bailey, John A. "Initiation and the Primal Woman in Genesis 2-3." *JBL* 89 (1970):137-50.

Ball, Ivan J. *A Rhetorical Study of Zephaniah*. Diss., Graduate Theological Union, 1972.

Bassett, F. W. "Noah's Nakedness and the Curse of Canaan: A Case of Incest?" *VT* 21 (1971):232-37.

Benito, C. A. *Enki and Ninmah and Enki and the World Order*. Diss., University of Pennsylvania, 1969.

Blenkinsopp, Joseph. *From Adam to Abraham*. London: Longman & Todd, 1965.

Boling, Robert. *Judges*. New York: Doubleday, 1976.

Booth, Wayne. *The Rhetoric of Fiction*. Chicago: University of Chicago Press, 1961.

———. *The Rhetoric of Irony*. Chicago: University of Chicago Press, 1974.

Brown, Raymond. *The Birth of the Messiah*. New York: Doubleday, 1977.

Brueggemann, Walter. "David and His Theologian." *CBQ* 30 (1968): 156-81.

Bullinger, E. W. *Companion Bible.* Part 1. Oxford: Oxford University Press, 1911.

Carmichael, Calum. *The Laws of Deuteronomy.* Ithaca: Cornell University Press, 1974.

Cassuto, Umberto. *From Adam to Noah: A Commentary on the First Chapters of Genesis I.* Jerusalem: Magnes, 1944.

———. *The Documentary Hypothesis and the Composition of the Pentateuch: Eight Lectures.* Jerusalem: Magnes, 1961.

———. *From Noah to Abraham: A Commentary on the First Chapters of Genesis II.* Jerusalem: Magnes, 1964.

———. *A Commentary on the Book of Exodus.* Jerusalem: Magnes, 1967.

Castellino, G. R. "Genesis IV, 7." *VT* 10 (1960):442-45.

Childs, B. S. "The Birth of Moses." *JBL* 84 (1965):109-22.

Clark, W. M. "The Animal Series in the Primaeval History." *VT* 18 (1968):433-49.

———. "The Flood and the Structure of Pre-patriarchal History." *ZAW* 81 (1971):186-87.

Clarke, Howard. *Homer's Readers.* Newark: University of Delaware Press, 1981.

Clines, D. J. A. "The Image of God in Man." *Tyndale Bulletin* 19 (1968):53-103.

———. "The Theology of the Flood Narrative." *Faith and Thought* 100 (1972):128-42.

———. *The Theme of the Pentateuch.* Sheffield: University Press, 1978.

Coats, George W. "An Exposition for the Wilderness Tradition." *VT* 21 (1971):232-37.

Cohen, H. H. *The Drunkenness of Noah.* Mobile: University of Alabama Press, 1974.

Crenshaw, James. "The Samson Saga," *ZAW* 86 (1974):470-503.

———. *Samson.* Atlanta: Mercer University Press, 1978.

Cross, Frank. *Canaanite Myth and Hebrew Epic.* Cambridge: Harvard University Press, 1973.

Crossman, J. D. "Judges." *Jerome Biblical Commentary.* Englewood Cliffs, N.J.: Prentice Hall, 1968.

Cundall, Arthur. *Judges.* London: Tyndale Press, 1968.

Dahlberg, Bruce. "On Recognizing the Unity of Genesis." *Theology Digest* 24 (1976):360-67.

Daube, David. *The Exodus Pattern.* London: Faber & Faber, 1963.

———. *The Duty of Procreation.* Edinburgh: Edinburgh University Press, 1982.

Davies, W. D. *The Gospel and the Sand.* Berkeley: University of California Press, 1974.

Driver, S. R. *Exodus.* Cambridge: Cambridge University Press, 1953.

Eissfeld, O. *The Old Testament: An Introduction.* New York: Harper & Row, 1965.

Evelyn-White, Hugh. *Hesiod.* Cambridge, Mass.: Harvard University Press, 1914.

Fish, Stanley. *Self-Consuming Artifacts.* Berkeley, University of California Press, 1972.

Fisher, Loren R. "The Patriarchal Cycles." In *Orient and Occident,* edited by H. Hossner, 59-65. Neukirchen-Vluyn: Butlow & Berker, 1973.

Flight, John. "The Nomadic Idea and Ideal in the Old Testament." *JBL* 42 (1932):158-226.

Fokkelman, J. P. *Narrative Art in Genesis.* Amsterdam: van Gorcum, 1975.

Frye, Northrop. *Anatomy of Criticism: Four Essays.* Princeton: Princeton University Press, 1954.

Frymer-Kensky, Tikva. "The Atrahasis Epic and its Significance for Understanding of Genesis 1-9." *Biblical Archeologist* 40 (1977): 147-55.

―――. "What the Babylonian Flood Stories Can and Cannot Teach Us about the Genesis Flood." *Biblical Archeology Review* 4 (1978):32-41.

Gerelman, Gillis. "The Song of Deborah in the Light of Stylistics." *VT* 1 (1951):168-80.

Gressmann, H. "Die Aufgaben der alttestamentlichen Forschung." *ZAW* 42 (1924):1-33.

Gilbert, Allan S. "Modern Nomads and Prehistoric Pastoralists: The Limits of Analogy." *JANES* 7 (1975):53-71.

Gordon, Cyrus. *Ugaritic Textbook.* Rome: Pontifical Biblical Institute, 1965.

Habel, Norman. *Literary Criticism of the Old Testament.* Philadelphia: Fortress Press, 1971.

Hallo, W. W. "Antediluvian Cities." *JCS* 23 (1971):57-67.

Hupfeld, Hermann. *Die Quellen der Genesis.* Berlin: Wiegendt & Grieben, 1853.

Iser, Wolfgang. *The Implied Reader.* Baltimore: Johns Hopkins University Press, 1974.

Jackson, J. J. and Kessler, Martin, eds. *Rhetorical Criticism.* Pittsburgh: Pickwick Press, 1974.

Jacobsen, Thorkild. *The Treasures of Darkness.* New Haven: Yale University Press, 1976.

Johnson, W. R. *Darkness Visible.* Berkeley: University of California Press, 1976.

Kikawada, Isaac M. "Two Notes on Eve." *JBL* 91 (1972):33-37.

―――. "The Shape of Genesis 11:1-9." In *Rhetorical Criticism,* edited by Jackson and Kessler.

―――. "Literary Convention of the Primaeval History." *Annual of Japanese Biblical Institute* 1 (1975):3-21.

—————. "The Irrigation of the Garden of Eden." *Actes du XXIXe Congres . . . des Orientalistes, Etudes Hebraiques.* (1975):29-33.

—————. "The Unity of Genesis 12:1-9." *Proceedings of the Sixth World Congress of Jewish Studies.* Jerusalem, 1977:229-35.

—————. *Literary Conventions Connected with Antediluvian Historiography.* Diss., University of California at Berkeley, 1979.

Kikawada, Isaac and Eric Hesse, "Jonah and Genesis 11-1." *Annual of Japanese Biblical Institute,* vol. 10 (1984), forthcoming.

Kilmer, Anne. "The Mesopotamian Concept of Overpopulation and its Solution as Reflected in the Mythology." *OR* 41 (1972):160-77.

—————. "Speculations on Umul, the First Baby." *AOAT* 25 (1976): 265-70.

—————. "A Note on an Overlooked Wordplay." *Zikir Sumim.* Leiden, the Netherlands: E. J. Brill, 1982.

—————. "How Was Queen Ereshkigal Fooled." *Ugarit-Forschungen* 3 (1971):299-309.

Kraeling, Emil. "The Significance and Origin of Genesis 6:1-4." *JANES* 6 (1947):193-203.

Kramer, Samuel. "The 'Babel of Tongues': A Sumerian Version." *JOAS* 88 (1968):108-11.

Kuhn, Thomas. *The Structure of Scientific Revolutions.* Chicago: University of Chicago Press, 1964.

Laessøe, Jørgen. "The Atrahasis Epic: A Babylonian History of Mankind." *BOr* 13 (1956):90-102.

Lambert, W. G. and A. R. Millard. *Atra-Hasis: The Babylonian Story of the Flood with The Sumerian Flood Story* by Miguel Civil. Oxford: Oxford University Press, 1969.

Lattimore, Richmond, trans. *The Iliad of Homer.* Chicago: University of Chicago Press, 1951.

Leach, Edmond. *Genesis as Myth and Other Essays.* London: Jonathan Cape, 1969.

Leichty, E. "Demons and Population Control." *Expedition* 13 (1971):22-26.

Lommel, H. "Die Yast's des Awesta." *Quellen der Religionsgeschichte* 15-6 (1927):198-203.

Lund, Nils Wilhelm. *Chiasmus in the New Testament.* Chapel Hill: University of North Carolina Press, 1942.

Malamat, Abraham. "King Lists of the Old Babylonian Period and Biblical Genealogies." *JOAS* 88 (1968):163-73.

Martin, James. *The Book of Judges.* Cambridge: Cambridge University Press, 1975.

McEvenue, Sean E. *The Narrative Style of the Priestly Writer.* Rome: Pontifical Biblical Institute, 1971.

McKenzie, J. L. "The Literary Characteristics of Genesis 2–3." *TS* 15 (1954):541-72.

McKenzie, R. "The Divine Soliloquies in Genesis." *CBQ* 17 (1955):157-66.

Muffs, J. "Abraham the Noble Warrior." *Abstracts: Sixth World Congress of Jewish Studies.* Jerusalem, 1973.

Nagler, Michael N. *Spontaneity and Tradition: A Study in Oral Art of Homer.* Berkeley: University of California Press, 1974.

Neilsen, E. *Oral Tradition: A Modern Problem in the Old Testament.* London: S.C.M. Press, 1954.

Noth, Martin. *Exodus.* Philadelphia: Westminster Press, 1962.

————. *A History of Pentateuchal Traditions.* Englewood Cliffs, N.J.: Prentice Hall, 1972.

O'Flaherty, Wendy. *Hindu Myths.* Harmondsworth, England: Penguin, 1975.

Petersen, David. "The Yahwist on the Flood." *VT* 26 (1976):438-46.

Pettinato, G. "Die Bestrafung des Menschengeschlects durch die Sintflut." *OR* 47 (1968):165-200.

Porter, J. R. "Samson's Riddle." *JTS* 15 (1967):106-9.

Pritchard, James, ed. *Ancient Near Eastern Texts.* Princeton: Princeton University Press, 1950.

Quinn, Arthur. *The Confidence of British Philosophers.* Leiden, the Netherlands: Brill, 1977.

————. "Meditating Tacitus." *QJS* 70 (1984):53-68.

————. *Figures of Speech.* Salt Lake City: Peregrine Smith, 1982.

————. *Broken Shore.* Salt Lake City: Peregrine Smith, 1981.

Rad, Gerhard von. *The Problem of the Hexateuch and Other Essays.* New York: McGraw-Hill, 1966.

————. *Genesis.* Philadelphia: Westminster Press, 1972.

Radday, Y. T. "Chiasm in Biblical Narrative." *Beth Mikra* 20-21 (1964):48-72.

————. "Chiasm in Tora." *Linguistica Biblica* 19 (1972):12-23.

Schadewaldt, Wolfgang. *Iliasstudien.* Leipzig: Hirzel, 1938.

Segal, M. H. "El, Elohim and YHWH in the Bible." *JQR* 46 (1955/56):89-115.

Simpson, C. A. *Composition of the Book of Judges.* Oxford: Oxford University Press, 1957.

Soden, W. von. "Die erste Tafel des altbabylonischen Atramhasis Mythus." *ZA* 68 (1978):50-94.

Soggin, J. A. *Judges.* Philadelphia: Westminster Press, 1981.

Speiser, E. A. *Oriental and Biblical Studies.* Philadelphia: University of Pennsylvania Press, 1967.

————. *Genesis.* New York: Doubleday, 1964.

Steiner, George and Fagles, Robert, ed. *Homer.* Englewood Cliffs, N.J.: Prentice Hall, 1962.

Tigay, Jeffrey H. *The Evolution of the Gilgamesh Epic.* Philadelphia: University of Pennsylvania Press, 1982.

Torczyner, Harry. "The Riddle in the Bible." *HUCA* (1924):125-49.

Toulmin, Steven and Goodfield, June. *The Discovery of Time*. New York: Harper & Row, 1965.

Weil, Simone. "The Iliad: A Poem of Force." *Intimations of Christianity Among the Ancient Greeks*. London: Routledge & Kegan Paul, 1957.

Wellhausen, Julius. *Prolegomena to the History of Ancient Israel*. New York: Meridian, 1957.

Wenham, Gordon J. "The Coherence of the Flood Narrative." *VT* 28 (1977):336-48.

Westermann, Claus. *Genesis 1–11*. Neukirchen-Vluyn: Neukirchen Verlag des Erzeihungs-vereins, 1966.

White, Hayden. *Metahistory*. Baltimore: Johns Hopkins University Press, 1973.

Whitman, Cedric. *Homer and the Heroic Tradition*. Cambridge, Mass.: Harvard University Press, 1958.

Williams, Gordon. *Technique and Ideas in the Aeneid*. New Haven: Yale University Press, 1983.

Wilson, Robert. *Genealogy and History in the Biblical World*. New Haven: Yale University Press, 1977.

Wolff, Fritz. *Die Heiligen Bucher der Parsen*. Strassburg: Trubner, 1910.

Yegerlehner, B. S. *Be Fruitful and Multiply*. Diss., Boston University, 1975.